The Simple Rules of Risk

Wiley Finance Series

An Introduction to Capital Markets: Products, Strategies, Participants
Andrew Chisholm

Swaps and Other Instruments
Richard Flavell

Securities Operational Management
Michael Simmons

Monte Carlo Methods in Finance
Peter Jäckel

Modeling and Measuring Operational Risk: A Quantitative Approach
Marcelo Cruz

Structured Products: A Complete Toolkit to Face Changing Financial Markets
Roberto Knop

Government Bond Markets in the Euro Zone
Analistas Financieros Internacionales

Building and Using Dynamic Interest Rate Models
Ken Kortanek and Vladimir Medvedev

Structured Equity Derivatives: The Definitive Guide to Exotic Options and Structured Notes
Harry Kat

Advanced Modelling in Finance
Mary Jackson and Mike Staunton

Operational Risk: Measurement and Modelling
Jack King

Advanced Credit Risk Analysis: Financial Approaches and Mathematical Models to Assess, Price and Manage Credit Risk
Didier Cossin and Hugues Pirotte

Dictionary of Financial Engineering
John F. Marshall

Pricing Financial Derivatives: The Finite Difference Method
Domingo A. Tavella and Curt Randall

Interest Rate Modelling
Jessica James and Nick Webber

Handbook of Hybrid Instruments: Convertible Bonds, Preferred Shares, Lyons, ELKS, DECS and Other Mandatory Convertible Notes
Izzy Nelken (ed.)

Options on Foreign Exchange, Revised Edition
David F. DeRosa

The Handbook of Equity Derivatives, Revised Edition
Jack Francis, William Toy and J. Gregg Whittaker

Volatility and Correlation in the Pricing of Equity, FX and Interest-Rate Options
Riccardo Rebonato

Risk Management and Analysis vol. 1: Measuring and Modelling Financial Risk
Carol Alexander (ed.)

Risk Management and Analysis vol. 2: New Markets and Products
Carol Alexander (ed.)

Credit Derivatives: A Guide to Instruments and Applications
Janet Tavakoli

Interest-Rate Option Models: Understanding, Analysing and Using Models for Exotic Interest-Rate Options (second edition)
Riccardo Rebonato

The Simple Rules of Risk

Revisiting the Art of Financial Risk Management

Erik Banks

JOHN WILEY & SONS, LTD

Telephone (+44) 1243 779777

Email (for orders and customer service enquiries): cs-books@wiley.co.uk
Visit our Home Page on www.wileyeurope.com or www.wiley.com

Other Wiley Editorial Offices

John Wiley & Sons Inc., 111 River Street, Hoboken, NJ 07030, USA

Jossey-Bass, 989 Market Street, San Francisco, CA 94103-1741, USA

Wiley-VCH Verlag GmbH, Boschstr. 12, D-69469 Weinheim, Germany

John Wiley & Sons Australia Ltd, 33 Park Road, Milton, Queensland 4064, Australia

John Wiley & Sons (Asia) Pte Ltd, 2 Clementi Loop #02-01, Jin Xing Distripark, Singapore 129809

John Wiley & Sons Canada Ltd, 22 Worcester Road, Etobicoke, Ontario, Canada M9W 1L1

Library of Congress Cataloging-in-Publication Data

Banks, Erik.
The simple rules of risk : revisiting the art of financial risk management / Erik Banks.
p. cm. — (Wiley finance series)
Includes bibliographical references and index.
ISBN 0-470-84774-3 (alk. paper)
1. Financial futures. 2. Risk management. I. Title. II. Series.
HG6024.3 .B36 2002
658.15′5—dc21 2002071302

British Library Cataloguing in Publication Data

A catalogue record for this book is available from the British Library

ISBN 0-470-84774-3

Typeset in 10/12pt Times by TechBooks, New Delhi, India
Printed and bound in Great Britain by Antony Rowe Ltd, Chippenham, Wiltshire
This book is printed on acid-free paper responsibly manufactured from sustainable forestry, in which at least two trees are planted for each one used for paper production.

Contents

Acknowledgements

I would like to express my gratitude to various individuals for their help in making *The Simple Rules of Risk* a reality.

My sincere thanks go to Samantha Whittaker, publishing editor at John Wiley and Sons, for her considerable efforts in supporting and guiding the project. As always, Sam has been a valuable partner and supporter. Thanks are also due to Carole Millett, editorial assistant at Wiley, for helping coordinate the mechanics of the project.

Professionally, I have had the good fortune of working for some of the best risk managers in the financial industry — I owe my gratitude to those who taught me, over a 15-year period, about the intricacies of the risk discipline. Specifically, I would like to thank William Lyman, Daniel Napoli, Steve Schulman and Richard Dunn for their efforts over the years. Each taught me a great deal about risk — including the importance of using common sense, prudence, judgment and experience when making risk decisions — and each guided me with enthusiasm. I am grateful for their friendship, support and instruction.

Patience, support and encouragement on the home front are vital in any writing project — as always, my wife Milena provided all three, and so deserves the biggest thanks of all!

Biography

Erik Banks has held senior risk management positions at several global financial institutions. In 2001 Mr. Banks joined XL Capital's weather/energy risk management subsidiary, Element Re, as Partner and Chief Risk Officer. Prior to that he spent 13 years at Merrill Lynch, where he was Managing Director of Corporate Risk Management, responsible for the firm's risk infrastructure; before that he spent 8 years abroad, managing Merrill's credit and market risk teams in London, Hong Kong and Tokyo. Prior to joining Merrill Lynch in 1988 he was a credit officer at Citibank and Manufacturers Hanover in New York. Mr. Banks is author of seven other books on risk, emerging markets, derivatives, merchant banking and electronic finance; he is also editor and co-author of a book on weather risk management, and is working on various new financial texts.

1 Introduction

1.1 RISK AND RISK MANAGEMENT

Risk, which can impact all areas of personal and corporate activity, can be defined as the uncertainty surrounding the outcome of a future event. In order to manage and control risks — to reduce or contain possible losses caused by uncertain future events — firms should strive to use all available tools and approaches. By doing so they minimize the chance that unacceptable losses will occur. Firms active in risk-taking businesses should seek to draw on both quantitative and qualitative approaches to help them manage their exposures. Quantitative risk management, which relies on mathematical models and techniques to identify, quantify and manage exposures, is one major approach to risk control; qualitative risk management, which focuses primarily on experience, judgment and common sense, represents a second major approach. Certain firms favor quantitative approaches over qualitative processes, while others prefer a qualitative focus; in some cases firms rely on both methods. Indeed, the "combined" approach may well be the best one, as the truly effective risk process draws on the strengths of quantitative and qualitative techniques to overcome individual shortcomings and weaknesses that characterize each discipline. As we shall note later in this chapter, qualitative approaches to risk management are periodically ignored in favor of purely quantitative techniques. The prudent firm must never forget that judgment, experience and common sense can be powerful tools in helping create a strong risk process. In this text we seek to demonstrate that the creation and application of qualitative methods of risk management — combined with relevant quantitative processes — can help a firm develop the strongest possible framework for managing the risks surrounding core business. Risk takers and risk managers must never forget that experience and judgment are powerful tools in the ongoing management of all risks.

Before embarking on a detailed discussion of risk rules we frame our discussion by reviewing quantitative and qualitative approaches to risk management, failures in the risk control process and diagnosis of control flaws. An understanding of these topics provides some insight into how many of the simple rules of risk discussed in the balance of the text are actually developed. To prepare, we digress briefly and review the scope of the risks considered in this book.

Risk management is the process of managing uncertainty that arises in the normal course of activities, including those related to business ventures. Business risks can assume many forms. From a financial perspective, these may include *credit risk*, or the risk that a counterparty will fail to perform as expected on a contractual obligation, leading to a loss; *market risk*, or the risk that movements in an underlying asset or index will create a loss; and *liquidity risk*, or the risk that assets cannot be liquidated or funding sources cannot be accessed without creating a loss. Each of these broad categories can be divided further. For instance, credit risk can be separated into default risk, settlement risk, sovereign risk, and so on. Market risk can be segregated into directional risk, volatility risk, basis risk, curve risk and correlation risk, among other categories. Other types of business risks can, of course, impact a firm, including *operational risk*, or the risk of loss due to flaws or failures in control processes, and *legal risk*, or the risk of loss due to errors in, or lack of, legal documentation; these can be decomposed into detailed subcategories. Various other types of risks can impact a company, including tax risk, strategic risk, business risk, reputational risk, and so on; in addition, non-financial operating risks, such as catastrophic property and casualty risk, business interruption risk and director liability risk, can create exposures and losses. While all of these are important, they are beyond the scope of this book and we will not consider them further. Figure 1.1 summarizes major types of business risks. A brief glossary of risk is highlighted in Table 1.1.

Each category of risk — regardless of its underlying characteristics — exposes a firm to the possibility of loss. The risk management discipline focuses on minimizing the possibility of loss, and limiting those that occur to "acceptable" levels. Though the term "acceptable" varies from firm to firm, we define it as a loss that is not significant enough to threaten the financial viability of an institution. Active management of risk, using all available approaches, is central to eliminating unacceptable losses.

1.2 QUALITATIVE AND QUANTITATIVE APPROACHES TO RISK MANAGEMENT

The management of financial business risks — particularly credit, market and liquidity risks — tends to evolve over time, as markets, products, skills and resources change. For instance, before the development and implementation of financial mathematics in the early 1970s, risk management was based largely on experience and judgment. The absence of sophisticated mathematical tools to help evaluate and analyze risks — apart from measures such as bond duration (developed in 1938), the Markowitz mean–variance framework (1952) and Sharpe's Capital Asset Pricing Model (1963) — meant that financial and corporate risk managers relied very heavily on common sense, experience and prudence in order to operate safely. Experienced line managers and financial controllers were responsible for decomposing risks thought to impact operations and developing rudimentary methods for managing exposures (e.g. broad risk limits constraining notional deal size); they often drew on experience from previous losses to help them identify and constrain potential "problem areas." There was little in the way of computing power to assist in the process — the technology focus was on mainframe-driven databases oriented primarily toward customer-related functions rather than financial analysis — and reporting of risk exposures was often manual. Given the preponderance of the "human element" — experience, judgment and common sense, supported by some basic numerical support — we might consider this a "qualitative" approach to risk management. While this method may not have prevented all financial losses, it was adequate given the environment of the time.

Markets in the mid-20th century were not as volatile as they have become over the past few decades. The collapse of the Bretton Woods Agreement in 1972, which had been implemented in the mid-1940s to create a system of fixed exchange rates, together with oil shocks in the early and late 1970s, which fuelled inflation and more active monetary policy initiatives, meant an increase in asset volatility. Currencies, interest rates and commodities began fluctuating by much greater amounts. Deregulation in the global financial and commodity markets during the late 1970s, 1980s and 1990s — including elimination of fixed brokerage commissions, removal of interest rate ceilings, passage of legislation allowing greater personal investment freedoms, erosion of the restrictions between commercial and investment banking, lowering of trade and capital barriers, and so on — translated into greater movement of capital across borders, markets and asset classes. The end result was, and continues to be, an increase in volatility — and a corresponding rise in financial risks.

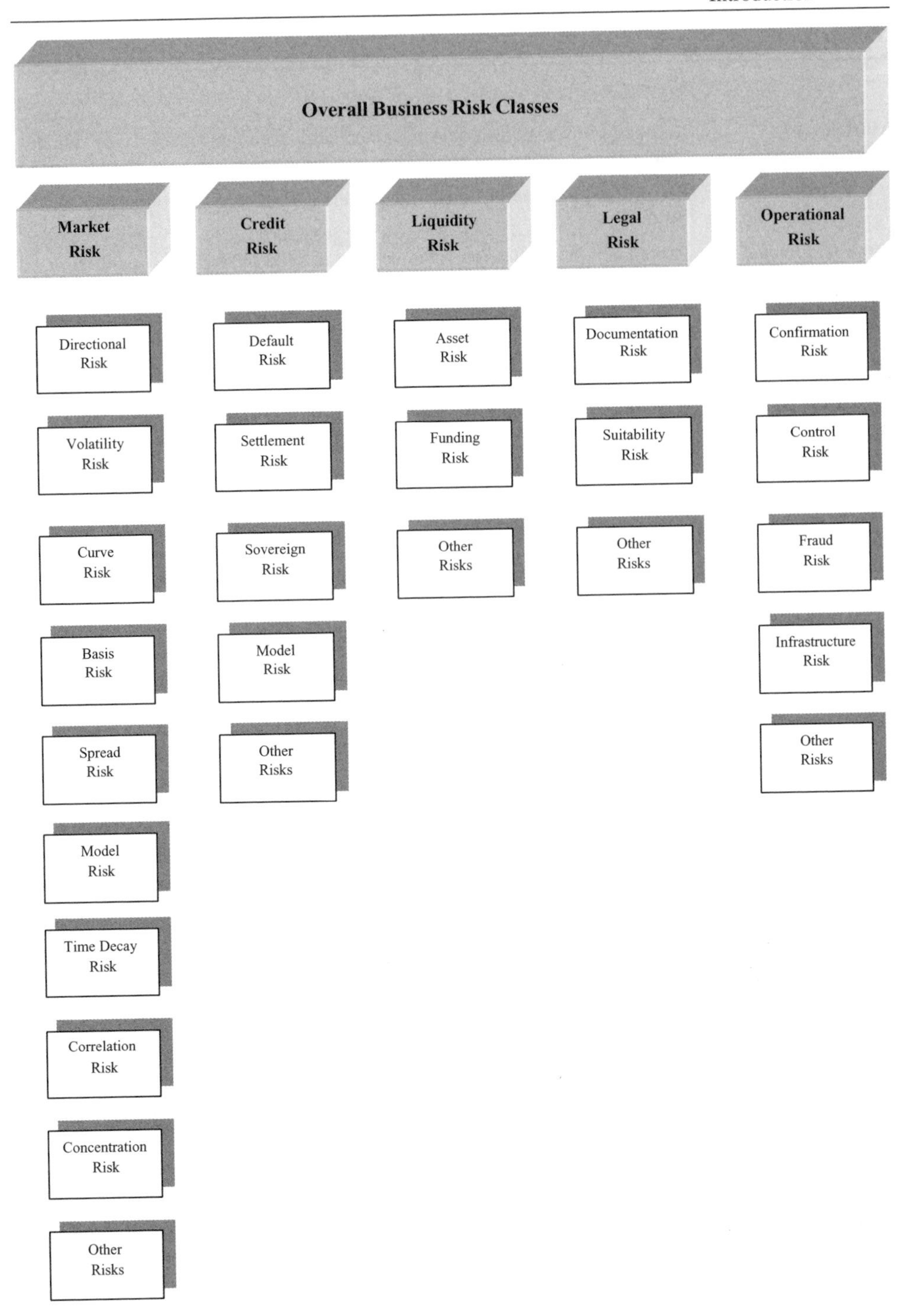

Figure 1.1 Financial business risk classes

Table 1.1 A brief glossary of risk[a]

Term	Definition
Market Risk	Risk of loss due to unfavorable movement in an underlying reference asset, index or market
Basis Risk	Risk of loss due to unfavorable movement between target instrument and hedge instrument
Concentration Risk	Risk of loss due to unfavorable movement in, or performance of, a concentrated risk position
Correlation Risk	Risk of loss due to changing magnitude/relationship of correlations between assets
Curve Risk	Risk of loss due to unfavorable movement in the shape of the reference curve
Directional Risk	Risk of loss due to unfavorable movement in the direction of the underlying reference asset, index or market
Model Risk	Risk of loss due to errors in the financial mathematics or assumptions underlying a model used for market risk management/valuation purposes
Spread Risk	Risk of loss due to unfavorable movement of a spread between two assets
Volatility Risk	Risk of loss due to unfavorable movement in volatility
Credit Risk	Risk of loss due to failure by a counterparty to perform on a contractual obligation
Default Risk	Risk of loss due to counterparty default
Model Risk	Risk of loss due to errors in the financial mathematics or assumptions underlying a model used for credit risk management/valuation purposes
Settlement Risk	Risk of loss due to failure by a counterparty to settle trade/cash flow
Sovereign Risk	Risk of loss due to sovereign action
Liquidity Risk	Risk of loss due to inability to liquidate assets or obtain funding
Asset Risk	Risk of loss due to inability to liquidate assets, risk positions or collateral
Funding Risk	Risk of loss due to inability to secure new funding or rollover existing funding
Legal Risk	Risk of loss due to legal events
Documentation Risk	Risk of loss due to errors in, or lack of, documentation
Suitability Risk	Risk of loss due to client suitability issues
Operational Risk	Risk of loss due to errors in processes and controls
Confirmation Risk	Risk of loss due to unconfirmed transactions
Control Risk	Risk of loss due to human error or lack of control over cash, securities and other assets
Fraud Risk	Risk of loss due to internal/external fraud
Infrastructure Risk	Risk of loss due to failure of internal/external infrastructure

[a] Risks can apply across a broad spectrum of asset classes, including currencies, equities, interest rates, commodities, credits, and so on.

As volatility began intensifying in the 1970s financial mathematics, the foundation of quantitative methods of financial valuation, trading and risk management, was moving into focus. Beginning with seminal work on option pricing by Black, Scholes and Merton in 1973 (followed by additional work by Cox and Ross in 1976, and many others during the 1980s and 1990s), quantitative methods for valuing and pricing a new generation of derivative instruments — financial contracts that derive their value from underlying references — gained rapid acceptance. Not coincidentally, exchanges were actively developing new risk management contracts at the same time, in order to protect against, or take advantage of, rising volatility. For instance, in 1972 the Chicago Mercantile Exchange formed the International Money Market to offer foreign exchange futures; in 1973 the Chicago Board of Trade created a sister organization, Chicago Board Options Exchange, to offer stock options. By the middle of the decade contracts were introduced on mortgage backed securities, Treasury securities and various physical commodities, and new contracts followed on a consistent basis throughout the 1980s and 1990s. The over-the-counter (OTC) financial risk management market, based on customized risk products between two parties, developed in the early 1980s through parallel loans; the structures were soon adapted to form generic interest rate swaps, a basic "building block" of the OTC market. Other derivative and structured products appeared throughout the 1980s and 1990s, including currency, equity, index, commodity and credit-linked swaps, options and notes; quantitative methods for pricing and managing the risks of these products appeared in tandem. For instance, in the mid-1980s large financial firms active in the bond market began using duration and convexity measures, bucketed by curve maturity, to limit their exposure to shifts or twists in the yield curve; likewise, corporate treasurers implemented asset–liability duration and bucketing to manage their interest rate sensitivities. By the early 1990s derivative dealers started valuing and risk-managing cross-asset risk exposures, including correlation and cross-gamma. During the mid- to late 1990s new quantitative portfolio risk measures, such as value-at-risk (VAR), credit VAR and stress testing, were created to give risk and trading managers information regarding their portfolio exposures.

Extension of quantitative processes has permitted the development of increasingly complex risk products over the past three decades. In some cases the availability of mathematical tools (and computing power) has enabled institutions to create new risk management products to solve corporate risk problems. In other cases institutions have developed products (or product frameworks) for their clients and then turned to quantitative analysts for pricing and risk management expertise. Financial mathematics have also been used to produce internal and regulatory risk management tools to help firms determine how much financial risk they have, or how portfolios of hedged risks are performing. The quantitative component of the risk process has been instrumental in allowing firms to analyze and manage their risks more efficiently and, in general, more wisely. Not surprisingly, the power and presence of "quantitative" risk management has moved steadily to the forefront since the early 1990s. Wall Street financial firms and others in the corporate world have attracted legions of quantitative specialists ("quants") — generally highly numerate PhDs from scientific or technical fields — who have helped transform the financial landscape by developing tools, algorithms, formulas and processes to create new derivative, financing and risk instruments. The availability of increasingly powerful, flexible and cheap computing resources has reinforced the process. Many of the mathematical processes now in common use, such as Monte Carlo simulation and binomial/trinomial option tree recombination, rely heavily on computing power. Quantitative approaches continue to spread throughout the financial and corporate worlds as a mechanism for creating, conducting and managing financial business and risks. For instance, quantitative teams, working in conjunction with their marketing and structuring colleagues, routinely develop new risk management products and strategies with complex pricing/risk management characteristics.

In order to properly market, value, trade and manage such risks, marketers, traders and independent risk officers require certain quantitative skills; such skills, at one time associated solely with derivative desks, are now found in many parts of an organization. For instance, a corporate bond desk might now have its own quantitative team to deal with the complexities of optionality in callable and putable securities and credit derivatives, while a mortgage desk might feature the same expertise in order to cope with issues related to prepayment speeds, option adjusted spreads, optimal hedges, and so on. The same is increasingly true in the corporate world. While traditional industrial and manufacturing companies were unlikely to have employed quantitative specialists a few years ago, many now feature such personnel in their treasury, funding and corporate risk departments. As a result, they are able to value their own risk portfolios, risk-manage their currency, commodity or interest rate exposures, "validate" pricing received from dealers and solicit terms for complex risk management strategies developed in-house.

In addition to "front line" use of quants to create, price and manage risk products, the internal risk and financial control functions at many organizations have come to rely on the same skill set. In the 1970s to early 1980s internal credit and market risk functions were staffed primarily by loan officers and ex-traders, respectively. Most of the approaches taken to controlling credit and market risks were fairly basic; knowledge of, and need for, financial mathematics, was limited — though growing. As product complexity increased the need for quantitative specialists within the independent risk functions (as well as associated areas, such as financial control) grew. By the 1990s it became common for large financial and corporate organizations to employ risk management quants in order to vet the risk of new products and develop quantitative risk measures related to potential credit exposures, derivative risk sensitivities, VAR, and so forth. Financial controllers, needing to independently value and verify complex risk structures, required and obtained similar skills. Such quants are now an integral part of most organizations and help ensure that expertise in the control structure keeps pace with that found on the "front line." Quantitative risk management is thus an integral part of the business unit and risk control process at many institutions, and will continue to play a key role in years to come. In some cases, however, institutions have over-emphasized quantitative approaches, causing fundamental "common sense" rules of risk management to be neglected. When this occurs, risk process failures can result.

1.3 FINANCIAL LOSSES AND FAILURES OF THE RISK PROCESS

On various occasions during the 1980s and 1990s basic risk practices and discipline slipped into the background. Strong bull markets and the profitability of risk-taking ventures, along with growing willingness to place greater faith in recommendations provided by models and quantitative processes, caused some firms to ignore many of the fundamental rules of risk management. As market dislocations, and associated losses, followed, a considerable amount of "post mortem" analysis went into discovering what had gone wrong. Failure to focus on basic risk processes was found to be a central cause of problems in many cases. While it is unlikely that qualitative approaches alone would have protected against all financial difficulties, it appears that proper implementation and use of basic risk discipline would have helped in certain situations.

Financial crises typically reveal problems, mistakes and weaknesses, and lessons on preventing future problems can often be drawn from these crises. Prudent companies follow such lessons diligently, while others may follow them for a period of time, until unpleasant memories have faded, and then revert to their previous behavior and practices; still others ignore the lessons entirely, carrying on as if nothing had occurred. Though financial crises have occurred regularly for many decades, even centuries, we need only review those which have appeared in the recent past to gain a general understanding of the nature of the risk process failures — valuable (and often expensive) lessons are contained in each crisis. For instance, following the asset inflation in Japan during the 1980s (fuelled, primarily, by loose monetary policy and imprudent lending standards), the bursting of the speculative asset bubble left hundreds of Japanese banks with hundreds of billions of dollars of bad loans. The banking system entered a massive write-off, restructuring and consolidation phase — a process that continues to the present time. Lessons related to the need for strong credit risk management, lending standards and internal controls abound from the Japanese experience. Many of the same lessons can be found in the Asian crisis of the late 1990s, where liberal monetary policy and speculative capital inflows led to sharp, and unsustainable, asset inflation; subsequent collapse caused significant regional bad debts, forcing the banking sectors of Indonesia, Thailand and Korea to be restructured and recapitalized; once again, lessons related to the need for prudent management of credit risks, leverage and credit concentrations are plentiful. Various crises in the mid- to late 1990s highlighted the linkages between financial markets and pointed out the frailties of credit and market risk controls. For instance, following the Mexican peso crisis (1994–1995), Asian currency crisis (1997) and Russian/hedge fund crisis (1998), many leading financial institutions that had significant market and credit exposures (such as CSFB, Goldman Sachs, Merrill Lynch and ING, among others) lost large amounts of money. Lessons related to the need for disciplined treatment of credit and market exposures, liquidity risk, collateral valuation and stress testing can be drawn from these episodes. Though the list of financial crises impacting the global system is quite large, a sampling of major dislocations that have occurred since the 1980s is featured in Table 1.2.

Individual corporate losses/defaults can also provide important lessons on failures of the risk process. As with broader macro-crises, the list of individual problems is extensive and varied; a very small sampling is illustrated in Table 1.3.

Table 1.2 Major financial dislocations

Year	Crisis
Mid-1980s	Latin debt crisis
Late 1980s/early 1990s	US savings and loan crisis
1987	Stock market crash
1990s	Japanese speculative asset deflation
1990	High yield bond crash
1992	European currency crisis
1994	US interest rate spike
1994–1995	Mexican peso crisis
1995	Latin American crisis
1997	Asian crisis
1998	Russian default/hedge fund crisis
1999	Brazilian crisis
2000–2001	Technology stock market crash

Table 1.3 Select individual financial losses

Entity	Loss
Local Authority Swaps (1986–1988)	£500MM swap loss
Drexel Burnham Lambert (1990)	Varied counterparty losses
Allied Lyons (1991)	£150MM FX options loss
Showa Shell Seikyu (1993)	¥165B forward foreign exchange loss
Procter and Gamble (1994)	$195MM leveraged interest rate product loss
Codelco (1994)	$200MM copper futures loss
Askin Capital (1994)	$600MM mortgage derivative/financing loss
Air Products and Chemicals (1994)	$113MM interest rate/currency derivative loss
Metallgesellschaft (1994)	$1.3B oil futures loss
Kashima Oil (1994)	$1.5B currency derivative loss
Orange County (1994)	$1.8B leveraged interest rate product loss
Glaxo (1994)	£130MM asset backed/derivative loss
Chemical Bank (1994)	$70MM currency derivative loss
Capital Corporate Fed Credit Union (1995)	$126MM mortgage derivative loss
Barings (1995)	£830MM index and interest rate futures loss
Daiwa Bank (1995)	$1.1B bond trading loss
Wisconsin Investment Board (1995)	$95MM currency/interest rate derivative loss
Postipankki (1995)	$110MM mortgage derivative loss
Sumitomo Corporation (1996)	$2.5B copper future loss
Long Term Capital Management (1998)	Varied market losses
Enron (2001)	Varied counterparty losses
Allied Irish Bank/Allfirst (2002)	$691MM foreign exchange loss

The list will, of course, expand as new crises strike. Despite learning from each successive dislocation, there will always be new lessons to consider, problems to solve and processes to strengthen. However, as firms learn from each crisis and use the lessons to create new, or strengthen existing, processes, the hope and expectation is that future losses will be minimized. While we do not wish to replicate much of the excellent work that has been done in analyzing these crises, it is helpful to consider several prominent institutional failures in order to illustrate basic flaws in risk processes that caused, or contributed to, losses. Though we simplify very complicated issues, valid summary conclusions can be drawn from each. These lessons provide important insight on how the lack of risk management focus can lead to financial problems. Indeed, some of the lessons from these failures contribute to the development of the rules discussed in this book.

1.3.1 Showa Shell Seikyu

Showa Shell Seikyu (SSS), a 50% owned subsidiary of Royal Dutch/Shell, is an importer, refiner and distributor of oil in Japan. As an importer paying dollars for crude oil, SSS has historically hedged a portion of its currency exposure using foreign exchange forwards. In 1989 the company entered into a series of forwards where it was required to buy dollars forward at an average rate of ¥145/$. Over the next few years the yen strengthened against the dollar. By the time the forwards matured, the currency was trading at ¥125/$, meaning that the company had a large loss on its forward position (but presumably a gain on its crude purchases, to the extent it operated a legitimate hedge program). Rather than recognize the losses, SSS's treasury department, apparently without approval, rolled over the forwards at historical, and by then well off-market, rates (in the form of "historical rate rollovers"). By doing so the losses were concealed in the new forwards; indeed, the banks involved in rolling over the contracts were effectively granting SSS loans to cover the losses. This process continued until the end of 1992, by which time the company had over $6.4B of forwards on its books. At that point, management revealed that total financial losses hidden through the contracts amounted to $1.4B, or 82% of shareholders equity — a significant amount given the size of the company. The practice was not, unfortunately, unique to SSS; other Japanese companies engaged in identical practices, generally with similar results.

Risk management lessons: any internal business unit capable of assuming risk must have its activities approved and independently monitored; dealing without appropriate approval in any type of instrument that generates a credit or market exposure can result in financial losses and should be regarded as an infraction of the control process; concealing a loss in hopes of "making it right" may lead to even greater losses and should be considered a violation of governance and control processes; financial controllers and auditors must be vigilant toward any practice that can result in the concealment of a loss or risk.

1.3.2 Procter and Gamble

In January 1993 consumer products company, Procter and Gamble (P&G) entered into a relationship with US banking firm Bankers Trust (BT, since acquired by Deutsche Bank) where it purchased derivatives structured by the bank. The company's apparent motivation was to use interest rate derivatives to help lower its funding costs; in the early 1990s it featured $5B of debt and had already executed certain simple, or "vanilla," derivative transactions. In November 1993 the company bought the first of several leveraged derivatives from BT. Most of the transactions were based on complex payout formulas that required P&G to pay BT increasing amounts as interest rates rose, and receive flows from BT (and thus lower its effective financing costs) as interest rates declined. P&G initially benefited as rates remained stable. In February 1994, however, the Federal Reserve commenced hiking interest rates, causing P&G to lose on its swaps. Indeed, the inaugural November 1993 trade required the company to pay 450 basis points (bp) over its commercial paper (or short-term funding) rate — a significant problem, and shock, for a company that hoped to use derivatives to lower its borrowing costs; in fact, the 450 bp premium was equal to an incremental $40MM of interest costs. By the time P&G arranged for BT to "lock in" rates on the leveraged deals in April 1994, it had accumulated $195MM in incremental financing costs. The company took a $157MM pre-tax charge on the transactions and, in October 1994, filed a lawsuit against the bank for failing to disclose important information related to the deals (such as how to compute the payout profile of the leveraged swaps under various scenarios), misrepresenting the risk of the transactions and breaching the fiduciary/advisory relationship. P&G noted that it was not the only end-use client to lose money from BT's sales of highly leveraged products — others had sustained similar losses, including Gibson Greetings, Sandoz, Jefferson Smurfit, Air Products, Sequa and Federal Paper Board, among others. The court case was accompanied by the disclosure of highly embarrassing material from the BT trading floor tapes, which reflected "aggressive" sales practices and attitudes by select BT employees. Prior to the conclusion of the court case the two parties reached an out-of-court settlement, with P&G agreeing to pay BT only $35MM of the $195MM due under the derivative contracts.

Risk management lessons (gained from both perspectives): an optimal hedge must be selected when trying to protect a balance sheet or income statement; leverage dramatically compounds the positive and negative effects of a risk position and must be factored into any trading/risk decision; a thorough understanding of the downside scenario of any risk position is vital, particularly under stress scenarios; the risks of a complex product must be thoroughly identified and understood; regular disclosure of risk to those who may be less capable of valuation is a sound practice.

1.3.3 Metallgesellschaft

Metallgesellschaft, a large German commodity and financial services firm, sustained significant losses through its US subsidiary, MG America (MGA), in 1994. Between 1991 and 1993 MGA sought to build up its US market presence and entered into long-term contracts with various counterparties where it agreed to supply 155MM barrels of oil products at fixed prices over five and 10-year terms; counterparties were also given the option of terminating contracts if market prices increased above the fixed prices. In order to hedge its risk, MGA entered into exchange-traded and OTC derivative contracts, including 55MM barrels equivalent in New York Mercantile Exchange (NYMEX) futures and 100–110MM barrels equivalent of OTC swaps and forwards. In order to manage its risk, MGA structured most of its hedges in the short-end of the curve, where liquidity was greatest. This hedging (known as a "stack and roll" strategy) necessitated constant rehedging as maturing contracts expired. In order to construct its hedge, MGA had to post margin on its exchange-traded hedges and collateral on its OTC trades.

Once the hedging program was underway, it became clear that the rehedging exercise would be difficult, as a significant number of contracts were needed to keep the position balanced; it also became evident that MGA was very exposed to the changing shape of the forward oil curve. As the value of spot crude oil fell, MGA found that the long-term contracts (a liability) were increasing in value, while the short-term hedges (an asset) were declining in value. Since the company marked its futures and OTC contracts to market — but did not do the same with its long-term forwards — it sustained large cash outflows; the losing hedges required MGA to post more margin with the exchange and more collateral with OTC counterparties, squeezing its liquidity. When it was finally unable to withstand the continuous cash outflows, it sold its hedges. As the spot price of crude recovered, the company sustained further losses on its unhedged position. The total loss attributable to the episode amounted to approximately $1.3B and resulted in a restructuring of the company.

Risk management lessons: a thorough understanding of how accounting conventions can affect valuations and risk behavior is vital; imperfect hedges can be extremely damaging; basis and curve risks are real and can generate losses; synchronizing time horizons is crucial in any hedging program; large, concentrated positions can create liquidity problems and may generate losses; financing margins and collateral is a requirement in many risk-taking strategies and must be factored into an overall funding program; failure to secure adequate financing in advance can lead to forced liquidation at the worst possible time.

1.3.4 Orange County

Orange County, a large county located in South California, operated an investment pool under the guidance of Robert Citron, the county treasurer. The pool invested proceeds on behalf of county institutions and organizations and, over a period of several years, posted very strong returns. Indeed, Citron's investment performance record was so strong that local school districts and other municipal entities in Orange County issued their own short-term debt and channeled proceeds to Citron for investment. By late 1993 Citron had $7.5B under management and, betting that interest rates would remain low (or decline), continued to amass larger interest rate positions, primarily in five-year agency securities. Citron made extensive use of repurchase agreements (e.g. buying securities and pledging them as collateral for more loans, using those loans to buy more securities, pledging those securities for more loans, and so on). He also purchased structured products with embedded leverage (e.g. notes with inverse floating coupons). The $7.5B of investable funds was leveraged to $20.5B, meaning that even a small increase in interest rates could have a damaging effect. In fact, when the Federal Reserve began raising rates in February 1994 (a process it continued for the balance of the year), Orange County's leveraged portfolio suffered massive losses. Though the duration (or average life and, hence, interest rate sensitivity) of the portfolio was only 2.74 years, the effects of 2.7 times leverage made the effective duration equal to 7.4 years — the portfolio was thus extremely sensitive to rate changes. By the end of 1994, after rates had risen by 300 bp, the portfolio sustained total losses of $1.6B — short of cash, the county was forced to declare bankruptcy and restructure its debt. The portfolio was liquidated and a spate of lawsuits commenced against those who had actively dealt with Citron. The municipal bond market in general suffered sharp price declines as investors began to search for excess leverage in other government investment portfolios; normal conditions did not return to the municipal market for many months. Unfortunately for Orange County, the liquidation of the portfolio coincided with a turn in the interest rate cycle — by the time the process was over, the Federal Reserve was back in an easing mode; indeed, rates dropped far more rapidly in 1995 than most expected. Several of the lawsuits emerging from the case were settled out of court; for example, Merrill Lynch pleaded "no contest" and agreed to pay $437MM as a settlement. However, the County's ultimate recoveries left it woefully short of its liabilities.

Risk management lessons: leverage can compound returns but may also compound risks; the lack of basic financial risk measures, which incorporate the effects of leverage and illiquidity, makes it difficult to manage a portfolio of risks; full disclosure of risks and returns to internal and external stakeholders is essential; concentrated, and leveraged, positions can damage individual institutions and broader markets; stress scenarios, focused on the seemingly "unthinkable," are an essential part of any risk process; client suitability issues can impact financial providers.

1.3.5 Barings

Barings, the British merchant bank that now forms part of the Dutch banking group ING, was the scene of considerable risk and control failures in the mid-1990s. Specifically, in 1992 Nick Leeson, a settlements specialist at Barings in London, moved to Singapore and soon assumed an additional role as an arbitrage trader, ostensibly capitalizing on discrepancies between the Nikkei 225 index futures contracts traded on the Singapore International Monetary Exchange and the Osaka Securities Exchange. In his capacity as an arbitrage trader Leeson was not permitted to sell options or take outright positions. In reality, however, he very quickly began taking outright positions and hiding them in an "error" account. Since no independence existed between the front- and back-offices — Leeson controlled both — he was able to disguise, over a two-year period, a growing number of outright, loss-making positions. Reporting was suppressed or altered in order to obtain funding necessary for exchange margins, and profits were inflated to make the arbitrage business appear very profitable.

The fiction continued through early 1995, when Leeson's positions began to grow so large that they became more difficult to disguise. The charade came to a halt following the January 1995 Kobe earthquake, which sent the Nikkei plunging and index volatility soaring. Prior to the earthquake Leeson had sold a large number of straddles (puts and calls with the same strike prices), taking in premium income and hoping the market would remain calm. The opposite happened, forcing Leeson to take larger outright bets. By late February, as margin calls increased and internal/external scrutiny intensified, Leeson fled the bank. The subsequent investigation revealed that Barings was technically insolvent, as £830MM of accumulated losses exceeded the firm's capital. The bank was ultimately subsumed by ING, which paid £1, plus assumption of liabilities, for the remaining assets. As the "post mortem" unfolded, the extent of Leeson's risk positions proved considerable: on a notional basis, he commanded \$7B of Nikkei futures, \$20B of Japanese Government Bond and Euroyen futures and \$6.7B of Nikkei straddles. Allowing for replacement cost factors (since the notional principal is not at risk in futures) the exposure was equal to 2.5 times Barings' total capital. The "fictionalization" of profits was also considerable. While Leeson claimed to have made £8.8MM in 1993, £28MM in 1994 and £18MM in early 1995, the reality was sharply different: he lost £21MM in 1993, £185MM in 1994 and £619MM in early 1995. Arbitrage businesses, which seek to take advantage of small price discrepancies, rarely produce such large profits — unless risk is being taken or results are being manipulated.

Risk management lessons: segregation of front- and back-office duties is essential, as is the existence of a strong, knowledgeable and independent risk management function; control officers (risk managers, auditors, controllers) must question circumstances where behavior is suspicious or explanations appear illogical; senior management must be actively involved in managing risk takers, wherever they reside; management must understand the nature of the business it is engaged in; profits and losses must be decomposed in detail by controllers to provide intelligence on how money is being made or lost; risk reporting must be produced independently and be of sufficient detail to provide relevant information; risk limits must exist to constrain activities.

1.3.6 Sumitomo Corporation

Like Barings, Sumitomo Corporation, one of Japan's largest industrial conglomerates, was the victim of very large losses that occurred primarily as a result of a breakdown in internal controls. The company, a large player in the global metals market, tasked Yasuo Hamanaka with building a metals trading capability in the early 1980s. Hamanaka became so successful at trading in the copper market (through the physical and OTC derivative markets, as well as the London Metal Exchange (LME)'s copper futures) that the company eventually gained a reputation as being one of the world's savviest and most powerful copper players. Indeed, as Hamanaka's influence grew, he became known as "Mr. 5%" for routinely being able to control 5% of the global copper market. Hamanaka apparently posted strong profits for Sumitomo, particularly between 1991 and 1995; as a result, he commanded considerable influence within the company. His success allowed him to remain in the copper trading role for many years, a process that is contrary to the rotation schemes practiced by most Japanese firms; over a period of years he built a team of copper traders around him, and gained control over all front- and back-office duties associated with his business.

Global copper prices began to weaken in the early part of 1996, as years of copper oversupply overwhelmed demand (e.g. average supply growth of 7% versus average demand growth of only 0.5%). At that point Hamanaka, who had successfully manipulated LME copper prices for at least six years (and perhaps as long as 10 years), had a very large long position in both physical and derivative copper that was highly vulnerable to a downturn in prices. As his attempts to drive the direction of prices became more obvious, regulators in the UK and US began making enquiries into his positions; almost simultaneously, Sumitomo launched an internal probe of its own and soon "promoted" Hamanaka out of the copper trading department. Hedge funds and other speculators, recognizing that Hamanaka's "promotion" meant irregularities, systematically drove down the price of copper over a four-week period, from \$2700 to \$2000/ton — much closer to equilibrium supply/demand clearing levels. As the internal investigation unfolded, it became apparent that Hamanaka, through control of both trading and back-office processes, as well as price manipulation/squeeze techniques on the LME, had managed to influence the copper market for several years. He was able to continue the fiction by having broad authority to trade significant amounts of copper (in the early 1990s he routinely accounted for 50% of LME's turnover) and keeping unauthorized deals in special accounts that were not recorded in the company's official records. Even when he was advised to reduce positions to 30% of LME's volume by internal managers, he used his special account to repurchase Sumitomo's own positions. Internal controls failed to detect any irregularities; since Hamanaka's early years were very profitable, he was given wide latitude to operate outside of traditional corporate practices. By the time the review unfolded, Sumitomo Corporation was forced to declare \$1.8B of losses, equal to approximately 10% of its equity; the figure was ultimately increased to \$2.5B.

Risk management lessons: As in the instance of Barings, segregation of front- and back-office duties is essential, as is the existence of a strong, independent risk management function; independent scrutiny of positions must be performed by an independent function capable of interpreting the risks; any time a significant share of an asset or market is under the control of a business, concentration risks must be reviewed and understood; profits and losses must be decomposed in detail by controllers to provide knowledge of how money is being made or lost; management must understand the nature of the business it is engaged in.

1.3.7 Long Term Capital Management (LTCM)

LTCM, a hedge fund, was founded in 1993 by John Meriwether and various ex-Salomon Brothers arbitrage traders (the fund also included option pricing pioneers Myron Scholes and Robert Merton as partners). LTCM based its investment strategies on relative value positions, such as convergence plays (theoretically "market neutral" strategies between two assets that are maintained until asset prices converge); the fund's relative value trades included on-the-run versus off-the-run Treasuries, callable bunds versus Deutschemark swaptions, and so on. LTCM also established certain directional positions, including a very large short position in equity volatility. In order to maximize returns, the fund employed significant amounts of leverage — though just how much was unclear until the fund unraveled in late 1998. Following its launch, LTCM quickly attracted large amounts of investment capital; by 1994, after it posted a strong performance, the fund had a total of \$7B of capital on which to build positions. In 1997 it returned \$2.7B to investors, but did not reduce positions — effectively increasing its leverage. By mid-1998, market turmoil in US interest rate products caused the fund to unwind certain positions at a loss. In August 1998, the Russian debt moratorium roiled the financial markets, causing a spike in volatility and a flight to quality — which converted convergence plays into divergence positions; all of these movements were detrimental to LTCM. On August 21 the fund reported losses of $550MM and, by the end of the month, increased the total to $2.1B. Attempts to raise new capital, which had declined to $2.3B, were fruitless. By mid-September the Federal Reserve became increasingly concerned about the systemic implications of a potential LTCM collapse — particularly after reviewing LTCM's portfolio, and discovering that its on-balance sheet leverage was already considerable at 30 times, while its off-balance sheet leverage was perhaps 10 times larger. All VAR and collateral liquidation stress testing was rendered ineffective by those seeking to quantify LTCM's exposures — this was an unprecedented multi-asset/market dislocation, well in excess of anything predicted by financial models. Another $500MM loss in late September caused the Federal Reserve and leading bankers to finally take action. Realizing that the collapse of LTCM threatened the viability of other financial institutions and, thereby, the financial markets at large, a "self-preservation" bailout group was formed. After several attempts at negotiating a rescue, 11 international banks agreed to contribute $300MM apiece to keep LTCM operating as a going concern (three others contributed smaller amounts). The management group was able to retain 10% of the fund, but a risk committee from the bailout group was tasked with the orderly liquidation of positions over a period of months. After some initial market jitters caused more losses, the environment stabilized and liquidation proceeded according to plan. By mid-1999 the 14 banks received $1B and were ultimately repaid in full. Meriwether eventually went on to form a new fund.

Risk management lessons: financial risk and trading models used to estimate exposures have limitations; stress testing of portfolios is vital, as the "unthinkable" tends to happen; collateral values can deteriorate rapidly, especially in an illiquid market; if an institution is extending credit to a high profile account, it is almost certain that others are doing the same — providing even greater leverage and magnifying potential losses; changes in correlation can increase the risk of positions; seemingly low risk trades (e.g. convergence/divergence trades) may not be as low risk as believed, particularly during times of market stress.

1.3.8 Enron

Enron, a large US energy company, was created from various small pipeline companies in the mid-1980s. Over the course of a decade it acquired more pipelines, expanded its operations into gas and power trading, and ultimately ventured into new areas it believed would benefit from market deregulation (e.g. water, broadband services, certain hard commodities). As the US power markets deregulated in the late 1990s Enron increasingly turned its efforts toward merchant trading, selling many of its physical assets (e.g. generation and pipeline) in the process. By 2000 the company derived most of its revenues from gas and power trading; indeed, its trading presence was so significant (i.e. 25% market share in certain energy sectors) that it became the seventh largest company in the world by revenues. In mid-2001, however, the company's growth began to slow and the value of its investments in areas such as water distribution and broadband services was called into question. In October 2001 the firm announced that it was bringing certain off-balance sheet items back onto its financial statements, causing a $1.2B reduction in its equity base; this move shocked many analysts, who were unaware of the company's off-balance sheet obligations. From that point on analysts, who had widely supported Enron's "asset light" trading model, began to scrutinize available financial information (in fact, Enron's financial disclosures had historically been very opaque, meaning credit and equity analysts, as well as bankers, were not necessarily making decisions based on all relevant information). As pressure built for the company's management to provide more information, new details came to light, including the fact that Enron had used multiple special purpose vehicles (SPVs) (with clever names such as JEDI, Chewco and Raptor) to move debt off-balance sheet and inflate earnings. As this information was disclosed the company was forced to restate five years' worth of earnings, causing the stock to plummet and rating agencies to downgrade the company's debt to one level above "junk" status. In order to assuage investors and creditors, Enron's CFO, Andrew Fastow, was fired and executive management was re-aligned. It was, however, too late: a liquidity crisis ensued and Enron was forced to post more collateral to keep its trading operations functioning; certain firms withdrew their credit lines entirely and the company began having more difficulty sourcing cash to sustain its businesses. By November 2001 the banking and investment community had effectively lost confidence in Enron and its management, and it became necessary for the company to seek a merger partner. An 11th hour merger agreement with cross-town rival Dynegy was struck; however, the agreement only lasted a few days and was cancelled by Dynegy after Enron's managers revealed new liabilities and rating agencies downgraded Enron to junk status (forcing it to post collateral that it did not have). Shortly thereafter Enron filed for bankruptcy, becoming the largest corporate failure in US history. Following the default many of Enron's executives (as well as its board members) claimed to be unaware of Fastow's actions, the creation of SPVs or the misstatement of earnings. Numerous congressional and legal actions began against Enron's management, a process that continued well into 2002; indeed, findings and actions may take several years to determine. Enron's auditors, Andersen, were also damaged by the disclosures, as they had effectively given the company a clean "bill of health" during the entire period; in the aftermath, Andersen lost a number of important audit clients and was found guilty of obstructing justice by destroying crucial Enron documents.

Risk management lessons: opaque or inadequate financial disclosure may ultimately lead credit providers, investors and rating agencies to lose confidence in a firm; when risk analysts are dissatisfied with management information they should question and probe until they are satisfied; a "credit cliff" (significant downgrading event) can lead to a liquidity spiral; lack of a robust and committed liquidity program can lead to significant funding losses and may ultimately lead to default; senior management and board members must not claim to be unaware, or be in a position where they are truly unaware, of a firm's financial activities; the ability to explain how profits and losses are generated is paramount.

1.3.9 Allfirst

Allfirst, a US bank subsidiary of Allied Irish Bank (AIB), was the scene of significant losses caused by John Rusnak, one of its foreign exchange traders. In February 2002 AIB announced that it had lost $691MM at its Baltimore-based subsidiary through the unauthorized currency trading activities of Rusnak. AIB's management indicated that, over a period of five years, the trader manipulated controls to hide losses in Allfirst's foreign exchange trading operation. Rusnak took dollar/yen positions well in excess of his authorized $2.5MM daily loss limit; when he began posting losses and violating limits, he attempted to cover up by creating fictitious trades. In particular, Rusnak booked fictitious hedges that made his book appear properly balanced and within risk limits, when it actually was not. Lax operational, financial and risk controls apparently permitted false trades to be accommodated (Rusnak was also permitted to trade from off-premises systems, contrary to most market and regulatory recommendations). Rusnak also engaged in certain high risk options strategies to help disguise losses; these ultimately compounded the damage. For instance, in order to generate cash to cover his losing positions, he sold deep-in-the-money currency options (e.g. he executed a $75MM trade with Bank of America through a prime broker account to cover a $50MM loss on spot positions);

while these brought in a significant amount of premium income, they were virtually certain to be exercised at a future time (requiring Allfirst to make a large payment to its counterparty) — this just delayed inevitable recognition of losses. As losses mounted it became increasingly difficult for him to disguise the positions; an internal investigation that commenced in mid-December 2001 eventually brought the problem to light. It is worth noting that other institutions in the dealer community expressed concern about Rusnak's activities and some even refused to deal with him; this information, however, was either not received, or not acted on, by Allfirst/AIB management. Risk control oversight by AIB over its subsidiary appears to have been minimal; Allfirst's treasury, responsible for foreign exchange trading, supplied basic risk information to AIB's Dublin-based risk control function (including the fictitious hedge positions), but scrutiny and control from head office appear not to have been strong.

Risk management lessons: an appropriate risk management/control system must be used to capture and monitor all trades and risks; risk-taking should not be permitted through off-premises systems; financial controllers need to verify and reconcile all positions and movements of cash; monitoring of risk activities in offshore subsidiaries by head office risk managers is essential; local managers must be responsible for the activities and oversight of their local employees; credit and market information related to a counterparty's activities should be shared whenever possible (within the confines of legal rules).

1.4 DIAGNOSING RISK PROCESS PROBLEMS

As noted through the brief examples above, valuable lessons can be gained by examining institutional risk management failures; by understanding how others have failed, firms can strengthen their own operations. To continue this theme, it is instructive to highlight some of the "telltale" warning signs that characterize flawed risk management processes; this can reveal possible problems and can be used to take corrective action — hopefully in advance of any losses. For ease, we consider flaws that can appear in each stage of the risk process. A typical process begins with a governance structure, which defines control responsibilities and authorities. It is followed by individual components of the risk management cycle, including identification, quantification, monitoring/reporting and ongoing management. Infrastructure, centered on technology and data, supports the entire risk process.

1.4.1 Flaws in Governance

- *The risk process is not independent of the business units it is attempting to control.* This indicates that no independent group of professionals is overseeing the risk-taking activities of the firm; those who take risk also monitor it, and do not necessarily impose limits/constraints when needed.
- *Senior/executive management does not understand the nature and/or magnitude of the risks it is taking*. This is indicative of a management team that is uncomfortable with risk, fails to understand the impact risk can have on operations, or views risk as unimportant or irrelevant in the larger scheme of business operations.
- *Accountability for risk-taking is ill defined.* This reflects problems with communication and potential unwillingness by those in the management chain to accept responsibility for the actions of those taking, or controlling, risk.
- *Management's expression of its risk appetite — in terms of types, amounts, markets, classes — is unclear and ill defined.* This, again, suggests an inability by management to

understand the nature and intricacies of risk-taking; the absence of clear expression suggests key executives are unable to grasp the essentials of the business.

- *Risk limits and policies are routinely violated without penalty.* This suggests that the risk control function lacks authority or management support and that management lacks control over those violating the rules. It also indicates that others in the governance structure, including executive management and the board of directors, are not discharging their fiduciary duties appropriately.
- *New products or commitments can be executed without prior approval or scrutiny by control functions.* This suggests that a formal process for vetting new risks does not exist and that entry into new markets, asset classes and instruments can proceed unchecked. It may also signal management's belief that new risks are not important enough to review in advance.
- *New risks appear on the firm's books without prior knowledge by those in the risk function or senior management.* This indicates disregard for risk policies/limits governing new types of risks, absence of policies designed to control new activities, or inability by senior management to control its business leaders.
- *Risk policies are vague and incomplete, and are routinely misinterpreted and "arbitraged" by businesses.* This indicates that the independent risk management function does not fully understand the nature of the business risks it is meant to be controlling or is unable to communicate directives clearly. It may also mean that business units have a disregard for policy and are willing to interpret rules in the broadest possible fashion.
- *Employees are unaware of general risk processes and regular internal risk education is not undertaken.* This suggests that managers do not feel broad knowledge of risk is a corporate imperative. It may also reflect a general lack of understanding regarding the importance of risk management.

1.4.2 Flaws in Identification and Measurement

- *Risks are not identified correctly.* This may indicate that the risk function is not given enough information to evaluate the risk of products and businesses, or that risk analysts are too junior or inexperienced to discern different types of risks.
- *The firm experiences losses that are greater than expected, or which are a complete surprise.* This suggests the independent risk function is unable to distinguish between different sources of risk or risk measurement analytics are too liberal in their underlying assumptions. It may also mean that risk limit structures are ineffective in controlling exposures.
- *Risk analytics used to compute exposures routinely underestimate or overestimate the amount of risk being taken.* This suggests the independent risk function is unable to understand the nature of underlying risk-bearing products or uses imprecise risk quantification methods.

1.4.3 Flaws in Reporting and Monitoring

- *Risk reporting cannot be done on a timely basis, or is routinely inaccurate.* This indicates that the firm lacks automated reporting processes, or that its central repository for aggregation and evaluation are incomplete. It may also indicate that risk analytics used to compute the value of specific risks are erroneous.
- *Regulatory risk reporting requirements cannot be met.* As above, this suggests the firm is unable to collate risk information in an automated fashion and distill it into the form required by different regulatory authorities.

- *Sources of profits and losses cannot be decomposed and monitored; the firm is unaware of how it makes or loses money and cannot attribute earnings to specific activities or risks.* This reflects a fundamental lack of understanding regarding the nature of the firm's business and how much risk is being taken, and whether different sources of business risk are profitable or unprofitable. It may also indicate problems with technological infrastructure.
- *Positions and trades cannot be reconciled to the firm's official books and records.* This may indicate deficiencies in the technological platform as well as the use of multiple sources of data to control a single business. It may also reflect ineffective audit and financial control processes.
- *Risk limits and decisions are not properly documented and provide no verifiable audit trail.* This suggests lack of discipline and procedure in basic risk policy and governance; it may also indicate an unwillingness by decision-makers to commit their decisions to writing.

1.4.4 Flaws in Management

- *Models and analytics are used blindly, without full comprehension of underlying assumptions.* This may indicate that senior management and risk managers are unaware of the power and complexity of models, their potential weaknesses and the general effects of model risk. It may also suggest that quantitative personnel are able to "intimidate" or "influence" those who might question or critique the underlying models.
- *Risk valuations are not tested or questioned.* This may reflect the presence of a weak financial control function that is unaware of the impact of potential misvaluations in a risk book or one that is easily influenced by risk takers and business managers. It may also suggest a willingness to accept a manager's view on the value of a position or risk, without question.
- *Backlogs of essential legal documentation are permitted to increase.* This may indicate lack of knowledge regarding the critical effect of legal documentation on risk exposures, presence of an understaffed/inexperienced legal department and/or absence of an automated mechanism for tracking past-due documentation. It may also indicate lack of knowledge or respect by the business units for the legal process.
- *The precise nature of collateral taken to secure trades cannot be verified; ongoing valuation of collateral is inaccurate and calls for additional collateral do not occur on a timely basis.* This might suggest the technology infrastructure is incapable of tracking collateral and sourcing automated price feeds. It may also indicate inexperienced settlements personnel who do not understand the critical nature of calling for additional collateral on a timely basis.
- *The exact legal counterparty to a trade cannot be verified with certainty.* This, again, may indicate flawed infrastructure. In addition, it may reflect a lack of understanding by business managers regarding the nature of their client relationships and the importance of identifying precise legal entities within a corporate structure.
- *Risk officers are not active/visible in the risk management process and are easily intimidated by business managers; experienced risk personnel do not form the bulk of the risk function.* This indicates the presence of a large number of junior risk personnel (perhaps administrators rather than managers) who do not possess the requisite knowledge and depth to work with, question or challenge business managers. It may also reflect senior management's unwillingness to spend resources on hiring more experienced, and qualified, risk professionals.
- *Risk managers are crippled by indecision; inaction on critical risk decisions occurs with frequency.* This suggests that risk management professionals do not possess sufficient risk,

product or market knowledge to make risk decisions, or are granted insufficient decision-making authority.

- *Business managers routinely appeal negative risk decisions.* This suggests that junior risk managers have little experience or decision-making authority, and are not held in high regard either by business managers or their own managers. It may also indicate senior risk officers are not capable of proper management and communication or wish to micro-manage the risk decision process.
- *Communication between risk officers and business managers is strained and counterproductive.* This might indicate lack of professional respect between the two groups. It might also indicate that risk officers are not visible and responsive, or that business managers violate or ignore risk processes frequently (without penalty).
- *Risk policies are not applied consistently.* This, again, indicates that risk personnel lack the experience needed to recognize that similar risks should be treated in a similar fashion. It may also indicate the presence of "favoritism" for some businesses over others, or the existence of ambiguous policies that are left open to wide interpretation and application.
- *The risk limit structure does not control the risks it is intended to constrain.* This may reflect problems in the identification and quantification of risks by risk personnel. It may also indicate that risk personnel are not sufficiently knowledgeable about the risks they are meant to be limiting and monitoring.
- *The firm has an excessively large market share of risk-sensitive business in certain sectors.* This may indicate the presence of flawed analytics and pricing tools (that consistently underprice risk), undisciplined risk takers who assume risk without understanding or caring about risk/return, or risk limit mechanisms that permit excessive risk to be taken.
- *The firm has excessive concentrations of risk in illiquid assets and long-term contracts.* This may reflect the fact that risk takers are not penalized for keeping assets on their books for long periods of time. It may also indicate the existence of a skewed compensation policy that allows risk takers to be paid for taking long-dated risks, with profits "present valued" to the current bonus period. As above, it may also reflect a liberal limit structure that does not effectively constrain risk concentrations.
- *Business managers are free to take and release discretionary reserves in their business lines.* This may indicate a weak financial control function that is unable to impose proper rules governing treatment of reserves. It may also indicate lack of senior management understanding on how the firm makes and loses money, and the types of risks it runs.

1.4.5 Flaws in Infrastructure

- *Significant manual "workarounds" exist to address shortcomings in the control process.* This indicates a lack of resources dedicated to the automated technology effort, a lack of understanding by senior management about the necessity of investing in technology and/or the ability for businesses to expand into new areas without creating proper infrastructure.
- *Risk takers are not required to input their risks into authorized systems.* This may indicate that management is unaware of the ramifications of an incomplete trading/risk population on its financial books, operational processes and risk reporting; it may also indicate that risk takers are able to circumvent systems requirements without notice or penalty, or that the firm lacks the resources to purchase or create a proper technology platform.
- *Off-system risks are permitted to grow without constraint.* This may indicate the firm is moving rapidly into complex businesses/risks that do not lend themselves to the functionality

provided by current systems. It also indicates that the governance process does not impose a strict new product standard and businesses can embark on new ventures without first implementing an operating plan.

- *Technological infrastructure is inflexible and incapable of keeping pace with business innovation and growth.* This suggests that the firm's technology platform is outdated and that resources for upgrading are not forthcoming. It also suggests that implementation of flexible technology designed to cope with changing products and markets is not seen as an internal priority.
- *Multiple sources of data are used to compute risk/financial/control information for a single business.* This suggests the firm continues to make do with legacy technology that draws information from multiple repositories. It also suggests that reconciliation processes are necessary or that erroneous information is being supplied to managers and decision makers.

These are, of course, only some of the risk process "warning signs" that can appear. It is fair to say that virtually every firm that is active in risk-taking has experienced some of these problems — few organizations can avoid difficulties as they expand and grow. Most firms are sophisticated and experienced enough to recognize a deficiency when it arises, and most are quick to resolve problems. Greater issues arise when numerous flaws plague a firm at the same time. In such cases it may be indicative of a general unwillingness, or inability, to solve the problems. In a risk-taking business inability to address control process issues greatly increases the chance that losses will occur; in the extreme, outright failure can follow.

1.5 STRENGTHENING RISK PRACTICES

New risk rules and regulations tend to emerge after financial crises. Though occasionally frustrating for those who have to adhere to new directives, the efforts are well intentioned and can be beneficial. For instance, in the aftermath of the LDC crisis of the mid-1980s, the Bank for International Settlement (BIS) established the BIS Capital Accord to set minimum capital standards. The credit standards were subsequently amended in 1992, and new market risk/VAR model amendments were introduced in 1996; consultative stages related to new credit models and operational risk modules commenced in the late 1990s/2000. These efforts are designed to ensure that the world's financial institutions have enough capital to support their credit, market, liquidity and operational risks. Following the derivative debacles of the mid-1990s (including those impacting P&G, Allied Lyons, Gibson Greetings, Air Products, and others), the Group of 30 (G30) released its voluntary "Derivatives Principles and Practices" guide, and the Derivatives Policy Group, comprised of leading financial institutions, created its "Framework for Voluntary Oversight;" both sought to create better internal derivative control and sales practice frameworks. After the LTCM debacle, a voluntary "blue ribbon" panel of risk experts from 12 top financial institutions[1] assembled to analyze what went wrong and what could be done to prevent the financial system from coming as close to a "meltdown" in the future. The end result was a series of prudent recommendations focused on fundamental risk management processes and procedures. While we will not review the recommendations in this book — though urge readers to do so — we summarize one very important observation. In particular, the group indicated that:

[1]Members: Goldman Sachs, Bear Stearns, Deutsche Bank, UBS, Morgan Stanley, Citibank, JP Morgan, Barclays, CSFB, Merrill Lynch, Lehman, Chase.

"Risk management is not simply a matter of better computer models to measure volatility and correlation more rapidly and precisely. Indeed, too much public focus has been placed on the sophistication and precision of risk estimation models, and not enough on the more important managerial and judgmental elements of a strong risk management framework. In the end, experience, market knowledge, management discipline, internal risk transparency and strong internal controls will be the more important determinants of how well financial institutions fare when the next storm comes."[2]

This thought echoes the theme we will explore at greater length throughout the book. In particular, an effective risk management process is one that is built on sound "common sense" rules. Many of these rules — which are based on judgment, experience, intuition, and other qualitative factors — are truly "art" rather than "science." Though they are not measured formulaically and cannot be quantified in any particular manner, they form the core of any prudent risk management process. In an era where quantitative risk management has moved to the forefront and become an important component of the risk process — rightly so — it is useful to recall and reinforce the simple rules of risk — rules that might be regarded as the art of risk management.

Effective risk management thus centers on a combination of quantitative and qualitative processes. The prudent risk manager, business manager, chief financial officer or chief executive officer should have as many tools as possible to protect against potential losses; this means that neither approach should be ignored or over-emphasized. Mathematical models cannot always quantify the exact price or risk of a structure, portfolio or business; equally, human judgment cannot always arrive at the correct risk decision or strategy. Together, however, they stand a better chance of producing the best possible answer or approach. The quantitative and qualitative intersect with some frequency in the world of risk management. The obvious place where this occurs, as we shall note later in the book, is in measuring and quantifying exposures. Risk managers, traders and bankers require quantitative tools in order to crystallize the economic impact of the exposures they are attempting to manage. The only practical way of doing so is to make use of the financial models that have been developed over the past years — even those with known limitations or flaws. As we shall discuss in Chapter 5, there is nothing wrong with using a financial model that is based on naïve or unrealistic assumptions, or that is limited in some fashion, as long as the shortcomings are recognized in advance and factored into the decision-making process. Quantitative and qualitative approaches can also come together in other areas. For instance, in monitoring and reporting risks, quantitative tools can be developed to produce reporting filters that provide an early indication of possible future problems — warnings that might not be readily apparent to the risk manager, absent some quantitative filter. Creating a true "best practices" risk framework therefore means uniting the quantitative and qualitative whenever it makes sense to do so.

1.6 THE SIMPLE RULES OF RISK

In order to create a top-tier risk framework, we propose that a firm can focus its efforts on applying certain "simple rules." Our aim in this text is to discuss the simple and obvious — though sometimes overlooked — rules that contribute to the effective management of risk; our aim is not to critique the quantitative aspects of risk management, as they form a core component of any risk process. Indeed, the two should be regarded as "partners" — where qualitative approaches fall short, or fail entirely, quantitative approaches can provide important

[2] "Improving Counterparty Risk Management Practices," June 1999, Counterparty Risk Management Policy Group, pp. 10–11.

solutions or answers; likewise, when quantitative approaches fail, qualitative approaches stand ready to strengthen the process.

This book addresses risk management rules that apply to a range of risks that a typical financial or corporate organization might encounter. As indicated earlier, risk comes in a variety of forms, and not all firms face the same types of risks. Financial firms may be very concerned with the market, liquidity and credit risks arising from their financial trading, derivative, financing and underwriting operations. Industrial corporations might be concerned about commodity input and output risks, funding and liquidity risks, and credit risks from their receivables. Municipalities might be concerned with any risk factor that can impact government finances, including interest rates, tax collections and public expenditures. Our intent is to express the simple rules of risk generically, so that they can be applied across a range of industries; however, given that risk-taking is often associated with the financial markets and the financial system at large, many of our examples and comments draw on concepts from the financial sector.

In the balance of this book we present a variety of rules related to the art of risk management; these are presented in some detail, in order to provide appropriate context and background, and to help illustrate why the rules are important. We find it helpful to consider the topic by dividing the rules into categories that reflect individual steps in the risk management process. We begin with rules that help define a firm's philosophy of risk. We then consider those that relate to the development of a governance structure; proper governance is vital, as it creates the framework around a firm's risk management beliefs and processes. Thereafter we turn to the individual steps that comprise a typical risk management process: identification, quantification, monitoring/reporting and management. Each step builds sequentially on the others — thus, in order to manage risks, a firm must be able to monitor and report them. Before it can monitor and report them, it must have mechanisms that quantify and measure them. And, before risks can be measured, they must be identified. We conclude with rules related to infrastructure. If governance defines the risk philosophy, "chain of command" and operating rules, infrastructure — based on data, technology, analytics and control documentation — mechanically and technically combines the components to create a cohesive risk platform.

1.6.1 The Cardinal Rules

The balance of this book focuses on a detailed presentation and discussion of simple rules that should form the core of any effective risk management process. To commence, we consider in summary form fundamental elements that are so important in any risk process that they should never be overlooked. We regard these as the 10 "cardinal rules" of risk management — the essential building blocks of any effective process; time and experience support the fact that these rules are vital in creating a strong risk framework. We highlight the fact that these cardinal rules span the broad steps of the risk process outlined above. This is by design, as the robust risk process features strength in every stage. The function is doomed to failure if governance, identification and reporting are strong, but management is weak. Likewise, poor infrastructure can render the entire process ineffective — regardless of the strength of identification, analytics and management.

The cardinal rules are thus based on the following:

- Risk capacity is not free and proper compensation must be obtained; the process should be disciplined and applied without exception.
- Human judgment is remarkably valuable; years of "crisis experience" can be far more valuable than recommendations generated by models.

- "Worst case scenarios" happen with considerable frequency in an era of volatility and event risk. The lessons of history — financial cycles and crises — provide useful risk management information.
- The risk governance structure should assign responsibility for risk to senior officials from various parts of the organization; officials must ultimately be accountable to the board of directors.
- Independence of the risk function must be undoubted.
- All dimensions of risk must be identified. Risks that might be less apparent at the time of analysis should not be ignored, as they can become more prominent as market conditions change.
- Models should not be used to the point of "blind faith" — they are only ancillary tools intended to supplement the risk process.
- The ability to relate profit and loss to risk, in detail, is paramount.
- Active management of asset and funding liquidity is vital in order to avoid potential losses.
- Data is the fundamental component of any risk process — bad data leads to bad information and bad risk decisions.

We believe that by considering these cardinal rules in conjunction with new or existing quantitative procedures, an institution with risk exposures can create a more efficient and effective risk management function; application of more detailed rules, contained in the individual chapters that follow, strengthens and deepens the process even further. Naturally, these rules do not eliminate the possibility of loss; eliminating loss, however, is not the function of risk management. Firms generally assume risk in order to earn a return, and thus expect to sustain some level of loss. But the rules cited above can help minimize the possibility of unexpected or "surprise" losses. If a firm has a properly functioning risk management mechanism, it then understands its risk, knows how much risk it has and how much it can lose under different scenarios; accordingly, it should not face any surprises by experiencing losses that are larger than expected or which come from unknown sources.

Obviously, creating a top-tier risk function requires considerable work and effort — including application of many of the other rules we present in the balance of this book. Though the rules we discuss are simple to understand in the context of a firm's business, a great deal of thought and effort must be devoted to the process in order to ensure proper implementation. Ultimately, this requires support and guidance from an organization's senior managers and executives, and must be sanctioned by the board of directors. When risk management is driven from the top down, it has every chance of being implemented successfully and followed diligently. If the commitment by senior management to effective risk management is weak, the process will ultimately fail. This eventuality can, and must, be avoided.

2
Philosophy of Risk

Before developing a process to identify, quantify, monitor and manage risk — indeed, before defining an overarching risk governance structure — a firm must establish its own view of risk tolerance and determine how it intends to attribute resources to managing risk. A firm must explore whether risk is an integral part of its business or a by-product to be minimized or eliminated; it must also establish whether it has the financial, human and technological resources to be an active risk taker and risk manager, or whether it prefers to use its resources in support of non-risk-bearing business. A firm should also assess whether directors and shareholders have a tolerance for risk, and whether risk bearing is part of the corporate mandate. Once these issues have been considered, the firm is able to create a "philosophy of risk" — essentially, an edict that defines how it perceives, and intends to manage, risk. As we might expect, these are very difficult issues that are often addressed incrementally, over an extended period of time. Few companies have the luxury of considering alternate approaches to risk and then defining appropriate operating boundaries; it is far more common to encounter a firm that already has risk exposure and must determine whether to preserve, expand or eliminate it.

Creating a philosophy of risk at the corporate level is a balancing of many forces — corporate goals, appetite, authority, economic profit, available resources, controls, and so on. For instance, if a firm is so risk averse that it wants no exposure in its operations, then no amount of economic incentive will persuade it to change its approach — it has effectively defined its philosophy of risk, and will do everything in its control to minimize or eliminate exposures. Likewise, if a firm is convinced that being an aggressive risk taker will allow it to meet its corporate goals and profit targets, it has defined its philosophy and must then support its strategy by hiring the best risk takers and risk managers, and developing the best risk technology. There is, of course, no single correct answer on how to define an approach to risk — it ultimately depends on individual corporate imperatives. Once a risk philosophy has been defined, however, the balance of the risk process can start to take shape. For firms choosing not to assume risk, sufficient controls to ensure elimination of risk exposure are necessary. For those opting to actively assume risk, the process becomes far more involved — a governance structure must be created, appropriate risk infrastructure needs to be deployed and a process of identification, measurement/quantification, monitoring/reporting and ongoing management must commence. Figure 2.1 illustrates the general risk process and flows for firms actively seeking to take risk.

2.1 RISK-TAKING SHOULD BE ALIGNED WITH OTHER CORPORATE PRIORITIES, DIRECTIVES AND INITIATIVES

When developing a philosophy of risk, a firm should ensure that plans related to risk-bearing activities coincide with, or complement, other aspects of corporate business. This means the firm should conduct a broad review of its operations and determine whether entering (or expanding

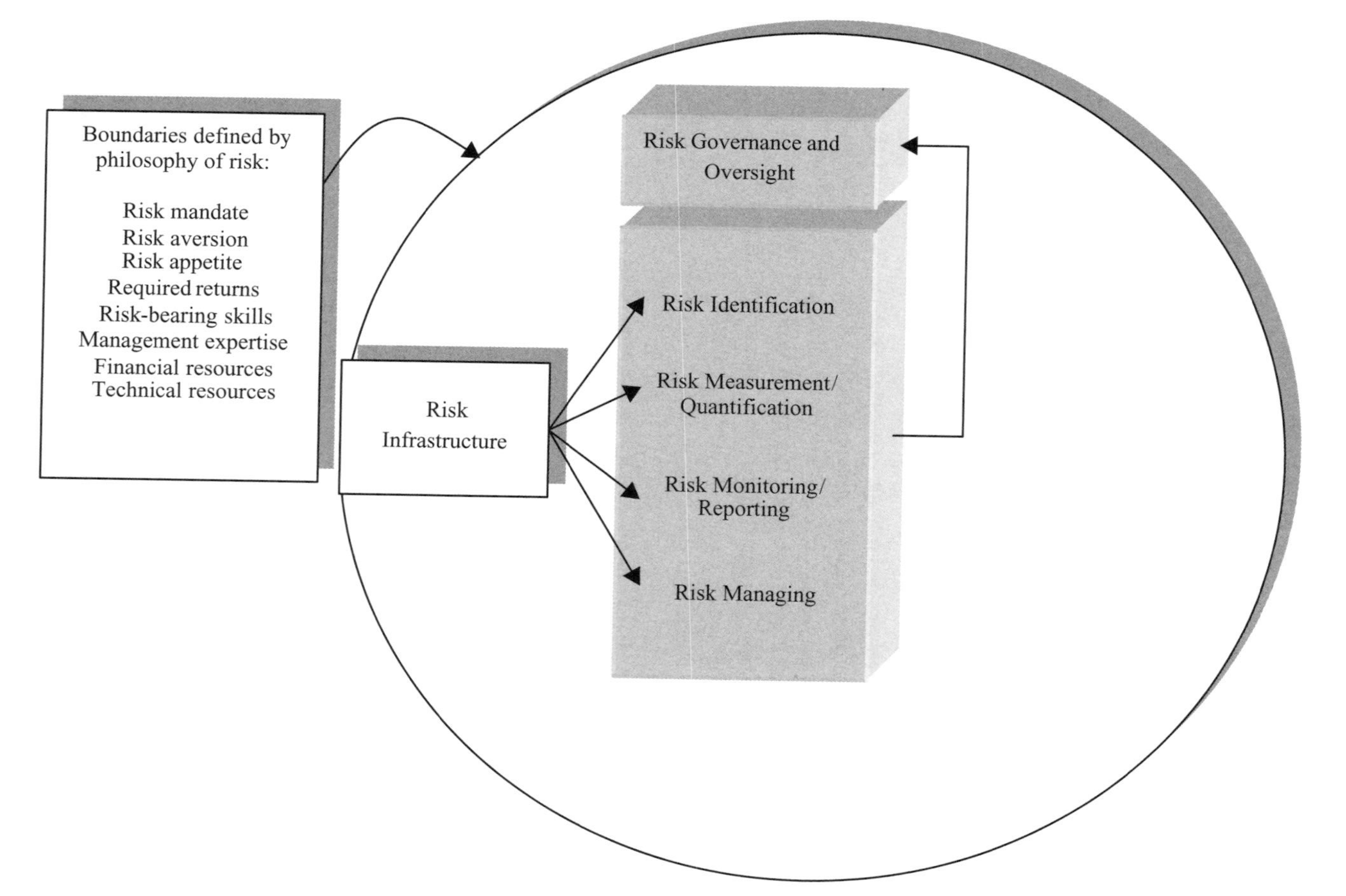

Figure 2.1 General risk process

within) the risk arena is consistent with corporate directives — and whether it will enhance, or detract, from other operations. For instance, if executive management of an auto manufacturer feels that establishing a dedicated, risk-taking treasury unit to actively manage the firm's exposure to interest rates and currencies would benefit corporate operations, it should determine whether the goal is consistent with its internal priorities and acceptable to corporate managers, directors and shareholders. Managers in the auto division may feel the initiative will detract from corporate resources, create unnecessary profit and loss volatility, consume management energies and divert attention from the core auto business; investors might feel the same way, and express dissatisfaction by selling the stock. If, in contrast, managers (and external stakeholders) feel the venture will provide greater financial expertise and diversify revenues, proceeding might be a wise course of action. Risk-taking ventures must therefore always be considered in the context of broader corporate imperatives. Taking risk for the sake of taking risk is never an advisable course of action; even if financial and technical resources are available to support such activity, risk-taking must still be consistent with a firm's business focus.

2.2 RISK SHOULD BE VIEWED ON AN ENTERPRISE-WIDE BASIS IN ORDER TO UNDERSTAND HOW IT IMPACTS THE ENTIRE ORGANIZATION

Though actual management of risks tends to occur at a desk, treasury or business unit level, a firm should review the totality of its risks when seeking to define a risk philosophy. By examining how aggregate risks — across broad risk classes — might act to help, or hurt, total operations, it can define its tolerance levels with greater accuracy and seek efficiencies in the management process. For instance, if a company is trying to create appropriate risk boundaries it should consider all of the financial and non-financial risks that might come into play. These might include commodity risk, interest rate risk and currency risk from a financial perspective and catastrophic property and casualty risk, business interruption risk and director's liability risk from a non-financial perspective. By understanding enterprise risks, the company might decide that some exposures can be mitigated while others cannot, some should be retained and others hedged away, and so forth. For institutions seeking to eliminate as much risk as possible, an enterprise view might reveal opportunities to improve on risk pricing through combined risk management mechanisms. An enterprise risk review can reveal important macro considerations during a critical point in the risk philosophy phase.

2.3 DECIDING TO BECOME AN ACTIVE RISK TAKER WITHOUT IMPLEMENTING A ROBUST RISK PROCESS IS LIKELY TO LEAD TO FINANCIAL LOSSES

Defining a philosophy of risk means ensuring that the requirements necessary to create a sound risk-taking environment are well understood. If a firm decides that it wants to actively assume risk it must be prepared to devote resources to the creation of a solid and effective risk management process. It can be financially damaging to underestimate the requirements needed for a strong risk process. A firm that does not fully appreciate the complexities might ignore particular stages in order to implement a framework more rapidly or cheaply. For example, a firm that wants to trade derivatives might hire a few experienced derivative traders and risk professionals, establish a risk committee, and mandate the creation of risk policies and limits. However, it might not invest in robust technology and data platforms and may thus develop a process weakness that could impact operations in the medium-term (e.g. perhaps the technology platform it purchases is not flexible or scalable, meaning that new products cannot be accommodated and will have to be managed and monitored in an error-prone "off-system" environment). A central component of any risk philosophy must include a definition of the resources needed to create a risk framework. When vital resources (e.g. time, capital, personnel, technology) appear inadequate, a firm may wish to reconsider its decision on risk-taking. Assuming risk without the correct risk process may ultimately lead to broader risk management problems and financial losses.

2.4 ACTIVELY ASSUMING RISK REQUIRES SUPPORT FROM KEY STAKEHOLDERS AND COMMITMENT OF NECESSARY FINANCIAL RESOURCES

A firm wishing to enter the risk-taking arena (either as a major risk participant or as one comfortable retaining, and managing, risk exposures generated by other core businesses) must ensure that it has proper commitment from key stakeholders and possesses sufficient financial resources to support the activities. In the first instance, a firm's board of directors and executive management should be convinced that risk-bearing is in the best interests of the firm and provide explicit support through a written corporate mandate. Determining whether risk-taking is appropriate is likely to occur after extensive analysis of core businesses, competitors, relative need for risk management, advantages/costs/benefits of participating, and so forth. Once a case has been made, the mandate received from internal governance parties, including the board of directors and executive management, must be explicit. The nature of the mandate should also be made known to those that have an external interest or stake in the firm's success — including bank creditors, rating agencies, investors and regulators. External stakeholders do not want to be surprised about a company's risk-taking activities — it is far better to advise them in advance rather than after the fact. The same should apply if a firm is already active in risk-taking but is changing its scope meaningfully.

As noted above, a firm must be certain that it has sufficient financial and technical resources to support risk activity. Risk-taking can be a capital-intensive business and those participating must understand precisely how much capital will be needed to support business during normal and stressed market conditions. It makes little sense to define an approach to risk, create a mandate, advise external stakeholders and then discover that during the first significant bout of volatility, insufficient capital exists to continue business. Resource requirements based on scenarios that reflect the seemingly "unthinkable" should be defined in advance.

2.5 RISK GENERATES PROFITS, AND CAN THEREFORE BENEFIT A FIRM — IT MUST, HOWEVER, BE MANAGED PROPERLY

Though risk is sometimes depicted in a negative light — often as an uncontrollable variable that creates losses and problems — the reality is far different. Properly managed risk can generate significant economic profits and serve as an important source of revenues. While "bad risk" — or risk that can expose an institution to loss without a proper level of compensation — is clearly not desirable, "good risk" — or risk that is properly valued and creates an appropriate economic return — can form the core of a valuable line of business. An industrial company that manufactures a product must manage all parts of the process efficiently in order to maximize profits; it attempts to control input prices, production costs and sales prices. If the company is successful it creates a good product with a good return; if it mismanages the effort by not charging enough for the product or paying too much for raw materials or labor, it has a bad product with a poor return. A risk-related business is no different. The risk-bearing company gets paid to take risks. In order to create good risk, it must charge enough for the product it delivers — in this case, risk capacity; such charges are the return on its "product." In addition, it must control its input costs (e.g. human resources, technology, product development efforts) and operate in a controlled manner; this, again, is no different than the industrial company. The key is to ensure that risk can be valued correctly and accommodated within a proper management framework.

2.6 RISK IS A FINITE RESOURCE THAT IS DRIVEN BY CAPITAL

The ability for a firm to assume risk is limited by the amount of economic capital it has at its disposal. A firm cannot simply decide to be a large risk taker, enter the financial arena, assume risk and continue to do so without limit. Shareholders supply a firm with capital by understanding the nature of the firm's business, how it makes money and how it plans to do so in the future. Capital is then allocated to risk activities. Shareholders will not, however, continue to provide equity capital without limit; though a firm may wish to access the equity markets in order to obtain more economic capital for risk-taking purposes, it cannot do so continuously. At some point the marginal return on risk will be inadequate, shareholders will become too diluted, the stock price will decline and it will no longer make economic sense to issue more capital. Accordingly, capital in support of risk-taking activities must be regarded as a finite resource. In deciding whether to enter the risk-taking arena, a firm must determine how much capital it can access and how it can best allocate it in order to maximize returns. The process must be reviewed on an ongoing basis to ensure that risk-taking, capital allocation and risk/return are proceeding according to plan. Thus, a firm entering a risky business by allocating an initial $10MM to the effort expects to earn a return on its allocation. If the business is successful, the firm may be able to allocate a further $10MM by accessing the public or private markets; again, it should receive an appropriate return for the capital employed. If the business remains successful, and the firm wishes to continue expanding but is unable to do so through the capital markets, it may then be required to divert existing capital supporting other businesses or curtail its risk-taking activities — it is simply unable to expand risk capital without limit.

Various concepts of capital exist and an institution must determine how to measure and manage its resources. At least two measures of capital — regulatory and management — can be considered. Regulatory capital is the total amount of capital a firm is required to maintain in order to fulfill regulatory requirements. Regulators impose minimum capital requirements on institutions operating in their jurisdictions in order to ensure a sufficient level of financial security to cover risks; this helps minimize the chance that institutions will take risks in excess of their financial resources. Firms identify the amount of regulatory capital required for the entire institution (e.g. based on pre-set formulas, percentage of risk assets, and so on), and then sub-allocate through a "top down" approach to individual businesses. Management capital, in contrast, applies the actual capital of the institution to individual businesses, often through a "bottom up" risk-related process. This helps ensure that each business has enough financial resources to cover the risks it is taking. Since allocations tend to be additive, and certain risks might be negatively correlated with others, an excess capital allocation can result. While these exist as separate, and sometimes divergent, measures of capital, they must be considered in the ongoing management of a company's resources.

2.7 RISK CAPACITY IS NOT FREE AND PROPER COMPENSATION MUST BE OBTAINED; THE PROCESS SHOULD BE DISCIPLINED AND APPLIED WITHOUT EXCEPTION

Earlier we noted that an appropriate level of compensation, or return, must be obtained in order to transform a bad risk into a good one. Just as the industrial company provides its customers with products at an appropriate price, so must a risk provider supply risk capacity at an appropriate price. A firm granting risk capacity to another market player must be fairly compensated for extending the risk, or the return required to support the internal allocation of risk capital will be insufficient — any methodical review of risk-adjusted returns will reveal a shortfall. In addition, if an appropriate price is not charged, participants will soon take advantage of the situation by obtaining as much underpriced risk capacity as possible from the firm — to the point where the firm has a misbalanced risk profile that generates more losses than gains. Identifying the market-clearing price of risk capacity is, however, only one dimension of the rule. Once market levels have been determined they must be applied, with strict discipline, to all risky businesses. Though there is a temptation (and even a practice) of underpricing risk in some businesses and overpricing in others (i.e. "loss leader" or "subsidy" approaches to winning business), this process is doomed to failure over the medium-term. An appropriate risk charge should be methodically levied on each piece of risk-sensitive business. Though this may result in the loss of some business to competitors who are willing to misprice their exposures (or who have different risk portfolio dynamics), it is a sound approach in the medium-term. Once "exceptions" start to occur, it is only a short time before mispriced risk appears on a regular basis.

The importance of properly pricing risk, and doing so in a disciplined fashion, is so central to the creation of a sound risk profile that it is considered one of the "cardinal rules."

2.8 MORE RISK SHOULD BE TAKEN WHEN IT MAKES SENSE TO DO SO — BUT ONLY IF THE REASONS ARE WELL ESTABLISHED AND THE RETURNS APPROPRIATE

Extending the concept above, it should be clear that there is a price for providing risk capacity. If the provider is properly compensated for supplying more risk, and if the risk is consistent with firm-wide imperatives, more risk should be assumed. For instance, if a firm has an opportunity to grant more credit risk to a particular client, it should do so as long as the exposures are within its overall tolerance and the incremental returns justify the use of capital. Though incremental, properly priced risk is often sensible, a firm will reach a threshold where it no longer makes economic sense to assume a marginal unit of risk — regardless of return. For instance, a firm that has extended credit to a client will eventually reach a point where it is imprudent to lend another dollar — even if the client is prepared to pay an attractive premium for the incremental capacity. (Note that in addition to internally imposed limits to prevent the over-extension of credit exposure to a single obligor, the existence of regulatory single lending limit rules acts as an additional constraint.)

2.9 A ROBUST RISK/RETURN FRAMEWORK SHOULD BE USED TO EVALUATE THE PERFORMANCE OF RISK-TAKING ACTIVITIES

A firm that contemplates risk-taking should create a framework that allows it to evaluate, on an ongoing basis, how risk capital is being allocated and how that allocation is performing. Since, as noted immediately above, risk is a finite resource, a firm needs to make sure that capital is being employed wisely by generating the highest possible returns for shareholders. A risk/return framework should be implemented to permit the firm to review, on an equal (or risk-adjusted) basis, the performance of individual risk-taking units. Thus, if a derivative desk and a bond desk each receive $100,000 of capital and the derivative desk generates a risk-adjusted return of $20,000 while the bond desk earns a risk-adjusted return of $2000, the firm may wish to consider reallocating some of the bond desk's capital in search of higher returns; when the bond desk's performance is better the capital can be reallocated. Such allocations and reallocations must, of course, be weighed against other corporate priorities and initiatives related to presence and activity in particular markets and should not be done "automatically." However, in a world of finite resources and demanding shareholders, a firm should create a framework to evaluate the risk and return generated by its businesses — and should be prepared to make adjustments as required.

2.10 RISK-TAKING SHOULD BE CONFINED TO AREAS IN WHICH A FIRM HAS TECHNICAL EXPERTISE AND A COMPETITIVE ADVANTAGE

Establishing a philosophy of risk means identifying the skills resident within the firm (or those that can be obtained externally and incorporated into the firm's culture) and using that expertise to create a core risk business. Expanding outside of that core expertise, if not done in a gradual, properly controlled fashion, can lead to financial difficulties or losses. Since managing risk in a volatile, dynamic marketplace demands considerable skills, those that choose to diversify into areas in which they have little or no experience risk losing money. For instance, if a firm devotes all of its resources to developing technical expertise in trading and risk-managing a European equity business, it may have no technical expertise or competitive advantage in trading US interest rate derivatives — the skills and experience required to successfully manage the interest rate business are entirely different. Entering the market without sufficient knowledge is likely to be an expensive proposition. If a firm wants to expand its risk-taking activities into new areas, it should do so by gradually building up its expertise or by hiring specialist teams and integrating them into the firm's overall business and risk processes.

2.11 "WORST CASE SCENARIOS" HAPPEN WITH CONSIDERABLE FREQUENCY IN AN ERA OF VOLATILITY AND EVENT RISK. THE LESSONS OF HISTORY — FINANCIAL CYCLES AND CRISES — PROVIDE USEFUL RISK INFORMATION

During the course of the past 20 years it has become apparent that "worst case" financial scenarios — low probability, high severity disaster events — have actually occurred with reasonable frequency. As highlighted in Chapter 1, events such as the Latin debt crisis of 1982, the global stock market crash of 1987, the junk bond crash of 1990, the European currency crisis of 1992, the Mexican peso crisis of 1994–1995, the Asian currency crisis of 1997, and the Russian default and collapse of LTCM of 1998 are examples of disaster events that have actually appeared with some regularity.[1] As the global financial markets continue to become more interrelated, there is every reason to believe that the volatility that has created past market dislocations will persist. Risk managers exposed to financial dislocations gain valuable experience by understanding how extreme market moves actually impact credit and market risk positions, market liquidity, collateral liquidation, mark-to-market valuations, funding limitations, and so on. An institution is well advised to use these "lessons of history" to help construct a risk management philosophy that allows it to assume and manage a portfolio of risks in stable and unstable markets. For instance, if a particular financial crisis demonstrates that liquidity can disappear rapidly, the value of collateral securing trades can erode suddenly, or high grade credit spreads can widen quickly and dramatically; a firm should use such information when defining its risk philosophy and creating a mandate for its risk takers. As a practical matter, when defining a risk philosophy a firm should review actual crisis events and apply these scenarios to the level of risk contemplated in each asset class; this provides an indication of the financial toll market volatility can have on risk-taking businesses.

Since lessons from actual historical worst-case scenarios can be used to help define a philosophy of risk, this becomes another of the "cardinal rules."

2.12 UNDERSTANDING THE DYNAMICS OF DIFFERENT RISK CLASSES CAN HELP DEFINE AN APPROACH TO RISK

Gaining an understanding of how different types of risks — credit, market, operational, legal — perform is important in helping define a risk philosophy. For instance, credit and market risks, though related, operate according to different parameters and time-sensitivities; it is therefore important to view them as two different disciplines. The immediacy of market risk decisions and actions is readily apparent. Since many institutions operate on a mark-to-market basis, where the day's results are effectively crystallized by revaluing profit and loss (P&L) and risk parameters based on closing prices or curves, the consequences of risk decisions are known instantly. In contrast, the results of a credit decision may take months, or even years, to determine. Since the credit decision centers on counterparty default as well as credit exposure generated through market movements, actual credit results are not known until the time of default or trade maturity — if long-term derivatives or loan transactions are involved, the results might not therefore be known for several years. The efficacy of the credit risk process must therefore be judged over a longer period of time. This means that market and credit risk officers must have different skill sets and should bring different perspectives to the decision-making process. It also means that senior management, seeking to define a firm's approach to risk, must be aware of the differences between these, and other, disciplines and determine which, if any, coincide with the philosophy being developed or expanded.

[1] The "fat tail" phenomenon indicates that financial prices may not be distributed normally (as many models assume) but with "fat tails" — suggesting that loss-making events happen with greater magnitude than is commonly assumed.

2.13 SENIOR MANAGEMENT SHOULD KNOW THE STRENGTHS, WEAKNESSES, MOTIVATIONS, EXPERTISE AND RISK BEHAVIOR OF ITS BUSINESS LEADERS AND RISK TAKERS

While managers need to be familiar with the skills and motivations of all of their employees, they must be especially attuned to those responsible for managing the firm's economic capital. Individuals who commit a firm to risk-bearing transactions play a special role within an organization — they have the power to enter into large, often multi-year, transactions that can generate significant financial exposures. Before allowing anyone to occupy such a role management needs to ensure that technical skills are undoubted and professional strengths, weaknesses and risk-taking behaviors are well understood. Certain risk takers are better than others; some are better as book-runners, others as managers of entire businesses. The best risk taker may fail when promoted to a trading or business management role, while a mediocre risk taker may excel as a trading manager. Understanding how personalities and skills figure in the management of a risk business is important in the business risk process; not only does a firm learn about the true capabilities of its personnel, but it can then allocate them optimally. Understanding the capabilities of business leaders and risk takers is critical in defining a philosophy of risk. Firms that discover they lack the necessary talent may decide to limit their risk activities until the skill set is strengthened; those that realize they have a talented team may decide to expand their risk horizons by entering new markets and products (though preferably in a gradual, controlled, fashion). Evaluation of skills should be a continuous process; management should strive to spend time with traders, trading managers, bankers and other business leaders on a regular basis.

2.14 HEALTHY SKEPTICISM — THOUGH NOT CYNICISM — CAN BE USEFUL IN CONSIDERING RISKS

Those active in the field of risk management are often skeptical by nature; this trait is generally deepened by years of dealing in a high-stress financial environment characterized by market dislocations, "disaster" events and large losses. Those with a certain amount of skepticism can assess the relative merits, risks and rewards of entering into new risk businesses by exploring worst case scenarios and refusing to accept the notion that a venture will be free of problems; they will demand comprehensive answers and force business managers to think through, and defend, their positions (or defer to the points raised). For instance, if a seasoned risk manager raises concerns about the relatively low level of profitability being generated in certain local fixed income/foreign exchange trades in relation to their potential devaluation risk, a review of past emerging market dislocations may support the skepticism. There is, however, a fine line between skepticism and cynicism; cynicism is counterproductive when considered in the context of business evaluation. An organization needs risk managers who add value to the process, rather than detract from it; those who view every risk with a cynical eye will create an environment characterized by negativity, mistrust, poor communication and lack of cooperation. While skepticism can be constructive, cynicism can damage the risk process.

2.15 THOUGH RISK ACTIVITIES OF FINANCIAL AND NON-FINANCIAL COMPANIES ARE BASED ON SIMILAR PRINCIPLES, THEY OFTEN FEATURE IMPORTANT DIFFERENCES THAT MUST BE THOROUGHLY UNDERSTOOD

The definition of a risk philosophy depends, in part, on legal and accounting rules that apply to firms in specific industries. Though financial and non-financial institutions can approach risk-taking in a similar manner — defining, for instance, what risks to assume, retain or mitigate, how much capital to commit to the risk process, what level of expertise to add in order to manage risks, and so on — each must then deal with issues that are sector-specific. For instance, financial institutions mark-to-market their risk portfolios on a daily basis, but not all non-financial institutions do so; many revalue their portfolios only periodically, and may select between the lower of historic cost or market value in assessing their economic worth. As such, measures that are based primarily on mark-to-market revaluations and daily or weekly liquidation periods (such as VAR) may not be applicable and alternate metrics may be required. In addition, the scope of product suitability may be different: while financial institutions are generally permitted to deal in a broad range of financial instruments in order to assume or manage risk, certain non-financial entities (including some municipalities and government authorities) may be restricted from dealing in certain instruments — this, again, causes differences in approach. These, and other, differences must be well understood when defining an overall risk philosophy, as they may create important boundaries, limitations or opportunities.

2.16 CREATING A RISK CAPABILITY AND PRESENCE SHOULD BE REGARDED AS A LONG-TERM ENDEAVOR

Deciding to actively take and manage risk is an important decision for any firm. If an institution decides that a certain amount of risk activity is consistent with its operations and overall corporate mandate, and it has the financial resources and management support to carry out the task, it must remain committed to the effort for the long-term; that is, it must support its risk venture for an extended period of time and resist the temptation to withdraw in the event of poor market conditions or bad risk results. Financial and time resources required to create or expand a risk venture are often significant: the time spent recruiting personnel and building infrastructure is generally considerable, and traders, business managers, risk managers and technology needed to support activities may be expensive. Accordingly, it makes little sense to view a risk-taking venture as a short-term operation that can be shut down after the first signs of negative news/results. Not only is withdrawal likely to be costly, it will send uncertain signals to external parties, including shareholders and regulators, who may question the firm's business management and strategic vision; this can have a damaging, and lasting, impact on the firm's reputation in the market. An institution deciding to take risk should be committed to doing so and view the process as a multi-year endeavor; a firm that is unsure of its commitment over a long-term horizon may wish to avoid the market, or enter it in a very minor and discreet manner. For instance, if a company believes that it wants to actively manage its own financial risks but is unsure whether it will remain involved over the medium-term, it may engage in a limited risk management effort by hiring a small team of traders and risk managers, confining its activities to very liquid listed risk products (with minimal credit, liquidity, legal and operational exposures), and purchasing an "off the shelf" technology package to value and track risks. If, after a few years of activity, the firm decides that it is comfortable with the risk-taking role, it can expand its scope and presence. Alternatively, if the venture proves unsuccessful it can exit the market with a minimum of expense, risk and publicity.

2.17 ONCE A RISK PHILOSOPHY IS DEFINED, IT SHOULD BE COMMUNICATED CLEARLY AND FOLLOWED WITH DISCIPLINE

When a firm concludes its analysis of all of the factors that influence the creation of a risk philosophy, it should communicate its decision clearly to internal and external stakeholders, so that all parties are aware of the nature and extent of proposed risk-taking activities. A clear definition sets the stage for subsequent steps in the risk management process, including the creation of a governance structure — indeed, governance requires a clear definition in order to function properly. Once a risk philosophy is defined it must be followed diligently. This means that the variables influencing the decision to preserve, reduce or increase active risk-taking should be monitored. For instance, if a particular amount of risk capital has been established for activities, then that minimum level of capital should be maintained. If hiring and retaining the best trading professionals forms an integral part of the philosophy, then the firm should ensure that the best traders are hired and retained. If the creation of an integrated credit/market risk team of professionals is deemed an essential requirement, then a combined team should be formed before risk-taking commences and should be preserved as long as risk-taking activities are in effect. If any of these underlying variables change (e.g. risk capital declines, trading professionals leave or the risk function fails to attract the right skill set) then the firm should revisit its philosophy of risk and revise it as necessary; the process should always be viewed as continuous.

Summarizing the simple rules related to the creation of a philosophy of risk, we note the following:

- Risk activities should be aligned with other corporate activities and should be confined to areas in which the firm has expertise and a competitive advantage.
- Risk activities must be based on a solid risk process and should receive appropriate commitment from all relevant internal and external shareholders.
- Risk-taking is ultimately dependent on the quality and quantity of financial and human resources; if either is lacking, it may be more appropriate to minimize risk.
- Risk is a finite resource, driven by capital, and must therefore command an appropriate return that can be measured through a robust risk/return framework.
- Taking more risk when a satisfactory return can be achieved is acceptable — underpricing risk is not.
- A firm's philosophy of risk must also be shaped by judgment, experience, skills and healthy skepticism; in addition, the skills and motivations of those intending to take risk must be well understood.
- In order to ensure that a firm's philosophy of risk is properly understood, the vision must be communicated clearly to all of those inside, and outside, the firm that have a stake in the process; as the market environment changes, the risk philosophy should be revisited and updated.
- Risk-taking must be regarded as a long-term endeavor, and a firm must be committed to supporting its activities over a multi-year horizon.

3

Risk Governance

Once a firm has developed a philosophy of risk it is ready to create a risk governance process. Governance permits articulation of the firm's risk mandate, establishment of a structure that provides for authority, delegation and accountability, and development of a control framework. This is especially vital for those seeking to preserve or expand their risk activities. Risk management cannot exist in a vacuum; in order to be an effective part of a corporation's processes and culture, management and communication links between the board of directors, executive managers, business units and control functions must be strong. The risk process must also feature links to external stakeholders, including investors, creditors, regulators and auditors. Risk governance must involve all relevant parties and should be sanctioned by the firm's leadership; there is little point in creating a risk control process if the underlying vision is not shared by senior executives, business managers and risk takers.

As noted below, proper risk governance — which requires active participation by the board of directors (to sanction the process), a risk committee (to guide the process), an independent risk management function (to manage the daily process), internal audit and other control functions (to audit and strengthen the process) — helps ensure that a firm develops a robust framework to control risks. Governance fosters continuous communication between senior management, business unit professionals and control personnel, and ensures that external parties are apprised of all relevant issues. It also injects clarity by defining the firm's total risk appetite across different risk classes, and sanctioning the development of, and adherence to, limits, policies and other control mechanisms. In the event of infraction or violation, it authorizes appropriate disciplinary action. A governance process can thus be regarded as the structure that gives a risk philosophy its shape and form. Though, as we note throughout the chapter, many aspects of governance can be clearly defined and delineated (e.g. the creation of committees, policies, limits, and so on) certain qualitative aspects help strengthen it — including consistency, communication, accountability, prudence, independence, knowledge, action, dynamism and discipline; although these can be difficult to measure, they are qualities that give governance its character. Figure 3.1 highlights a sample governance process.

As noted, a risk process cannot function properly without clear governance. The lack of separation between front- and back-office activities and the failure of market/credit risk controls are just two of the many by-products of an ill-defined governance process. As noted in Chapter 1, Barings was brought down by internal fraud stemming from lack of independence between trading and settlements; much the same occurred at Sumitomo Corporation and Daiwa Bank. Such failures renewed the call for independence between front- and back-office activities, a practice that most firms have started to follow. Failure in governance has also been demonstrated by large market and credit risk losses. For instance, during the 1998 Russian/LTCM crisis, numerous financial institutions sustained significant losses by ignoring

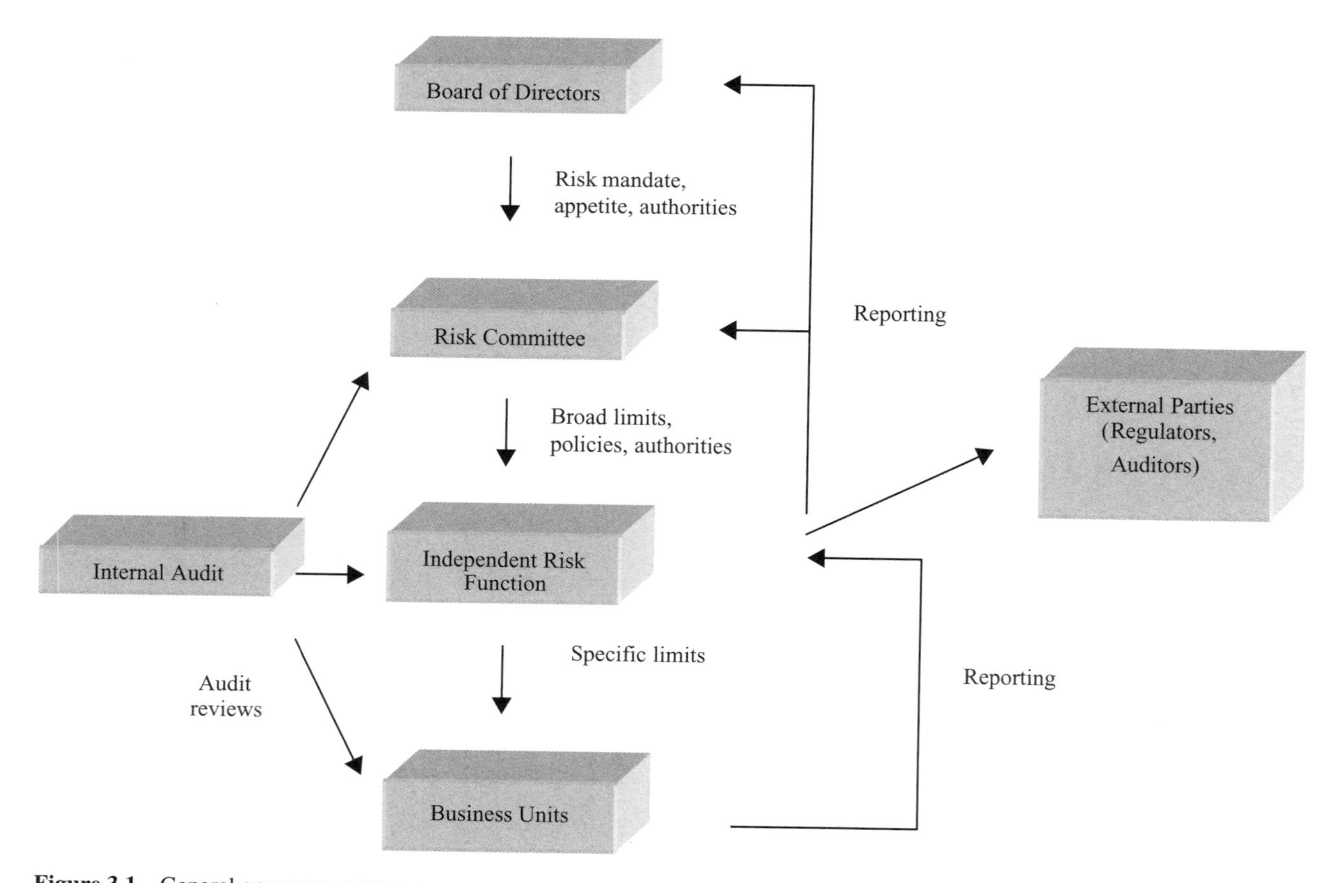

Figure 3.1 General governance process

fundamental risk procedures and practices. The losses led to calls for clearer definitions and expressions of risk appetite, renewed focus on credit and market risk exposures under stress scenarios (particularly those based on leverage and illiquidity), and improved management of liquidity and collateral. Such control and risk lessons must be incorporated into the governance process in order to strengthen it over time.

3.1 RISK CLASSES NEED TO BE CLEARLY DEFINED AND DELINEATED

In order to establish a firm's risk appetite it is important to define the different categories of risk that might arise in the normal course of business. Risk is complex, and can assume many forms (an issue we consider at greater length in Chapter 4); care must be taken to ensure that those in the governance process understand, and distinguish between, various risk categories. For instance, a firm may wish to divide its market risk exposure into categories such as directional risk, volatility risk, spread risk, basis risk, correlation risk, and so on. In the credit risk sector, it might differentiate between loan and derivative credit default risk, settlement risk, sovereign risk, and so on. Regardless of the granularity of the categories, there should be agreement between the governance parties on how risk is defined/classed and then limited; the board should sanction all such decisions. Since risk classes can change over time as new products, markets and participants are introduced, classifications should be amended as necessary.

3.2 CLEAR EXPRESSION OF FIRM-WIDE RISK APPETITE IS ESSENTIAL

One of the most critical functions of the governance process is ensuring proper communication of risk tolerance levels. The board of directors, risk committee and senior risk officer must express the firm's risk appetite to all relevant parties clearly — there can be no room for confusion or misinterpretation. For instance, if the firm's tolerance for sub-investment grade credit risk exposure is defined to be a certain amount and its tolerance for market risk resulting from the movement of US interest rates is some other amount, then such tolerance levels must be memorialized and communicated through the governance chain. The board should provide, and then communicate, such authority to the risk committee; the risk committee and risk management function must ensure that all business unit leaders understand the nature of the firm's risk capacity, how it is measured and what it means. If the risk process is operating properly, senior business and control leaders should have a clear notion of how much risk the firm is willing to take in different asset classes and with different counterparties. If confusion exists, then there is a good chance that risk appetite has not been well defined or properly articulated; immediate clarification is then essential. As in any dynamic process, risk capacity changes as market opportunities, conditions and circumstances change; accordingly, it is helpful to communicate the firm's risk appetite on a continuous basis — even when there is no change. This can take the form of monthly or quarterly updates by the risk committee to a broad audience of business and control managers, or some alternate form; regardless of the forum or mechanism, a regular communiqué is advisable.

3.3 THE RISK GOVERNANCE STRUCTURE SHOULD ASSIGN RESPONSIBILITY FOR RISK TO SENIOR OFFICIALS FROM VARIOUS PARTS OF THE ORGANIZATION; THESE OFFICIALS MUST ULTIMATELY BE ACCOUNTABLE TO THE BOARD OF DIRECTORS

Institutions developing or restructuring their risk organizations are able to select from various approaches and structures. While some choose to create risk functions within broader financial/control organizations (e.g. the chief financial office), others may decide to form dedicated units that report directly to executive management. In fact, the actual construct and organization is less important than the governance structure surrounding the function. A proper governance structure draws in leadership from various parts of the firm and assigns accountability at all levels — including executive managers, business unit leaders and risk officers. The governance structure sanctioned by the board must be empowered and accountable, and should include a diverse group of senior managers; this helps ensure proper skills are on hand to manage the allocation of risk resources and that the process cannot be guided or influenced by a single constituency.

In a typical risk governance structure, the board of directors, having been advised by executive management on the firm's intended approach to risk (and having also consulted with key external parties, such as regulators and rating agencies), might create a risk mandate which defines the risk appetite and operating parameters, and sanctions the creation of a risk committee and risk controls/policies; the mandate may also delegate specific risk authorities to senior officials. A risk committee, chaired by the senior risk officer and comprised of senior business unit and control managers, might be charged by the board with creating a risk process that includes development of risk policies and establishment of high level risk limits (that reflect the firm's risk appetite). The risk committee may delegate risk authorities to the senior risk officer, in his or her role as head of the firm's independent risk management function. The senior risk officer, in turn, may sub-allocate risk authorities to senior market and credit risk deputies, who can then exercise decision-making authority within set parameters. Assuming risks in excess of authorities should, in most instances, be elevated through the governance structure. The senior risk officer may be given authority by the risk committee to exceed pre-established limits by a certain percentage without first reporting back to the committee. The committee itself might be granted similar approval authority by the board of directors. Any requests in excess of a priori approval levels might require a subgroup of the board of directors to convene. This type of approach ensures that the governance structure is flexible enough to accommodate the demands of a fast-moving marketplace, where the need to assume risk on a "short-fuse" basis is real. However, it also instills discipline and accountability by ensuring that the board of directors and risk committee are aware of, and accountable for, risks. The board must have ultimate accountability. In addition to establishing risk appetite, limits and policies, the governance structure should permit the creation and use of other risk bodies/committees, including those responsible for drafting risk policies, valuing complex risks, establishing risk-related reserves, considering new risk-bearing products or reviewing risk-based capital commitments. These bodies, which can help facilitate implementation of the risk process, may be directly accountable to the risk committee.

In order for the governance structure to perform as intended, communication must flow downwards and upwards. The board and risk committee must regularly communicate the firm's risk imperatives, as well as any changes in its risk philosophy. The senior risk officer, in turn, must regularly advise the risk committee and the board of all relevant risk-related matters that might impact the firm's performance, including exposures, violations of the control process, and so on. To verify that the process is working as intended, the internal audit group should audit different aspects of the governance process on a periodic basis.

The creation of a proper governance structure, with senior executive representation from a range of functions and business lines, is so instrumental to the development of a risk process that it becomes one of the "cardinal rules."

3.4 ACCOUNTABILITY FOR RISK MUST RUN FROM THE TOP TO THE BOTTOM OF AN ORGANIZATION; SENIOR MANAGEMENT MUST NOT CLAIM TO BE UNAWARE OF RISK, OR BE IN A POSITION WHERE THEY ARE UNAWARE OF RISK

Accountability for actions is one of the central purposes of any risk governance structure. There is no point in delegating risk authorities through a hierarchical chain and requiring updates on risk exposures if members of the governance structure are not held accountable for their roles in the process. It is disingenuous, for instance, for board members or senior executives to allocate capital for emerging markets risk, receive briefings on the level of exposure from the risk committee, and then claim ignorance or surprise when an emerging market dislocation causes a loss (that falls within the firm's predefined tolerance levels). This is unsatisfactory and a sign that duties are not being discharged properly. The same applies to others in the risk governance structure — from the risk committee down to senior and junior risk officers; each is vested with certain corporate responsibility and authority, and must discharge duties with care and precision — and full accountability. Failure to act prudently in discharging duties should be regarded as a serious, and unacceptable, breach. Members of the governance process must not, of course, be in a position where they are unaware of risks. This indicates a process breakdown on at least two fronts: inadequate risk reporting/communication from the bottom up, and inadequate knowledge of the firm's risk-bearing business from the top down. For instance, if the board of directors and risk committee specifically approve risk-taking in emerging markets, and weekly risk updates fail to highlight the presence of emerging market risk exposures, a loss sustained in that market should come as a surprise to senior executives and board members — though the risk may have been approved through the governance process, failure to report on actual risks (and subsequent losses) leaves directors unaware of risk. Corrective actions must be implemented without delay.

3.5 HUMAN JUDGMENT IS REMARKABLY VALUABLE; YEARS OF "CRISIS EXPERIENCE" CAN BE FAR MORE VALUABLE THAN RECOMMENDATIONS GENERATED BY MODELS

As indicated in Chapter 1, advances in computing power and modeling/analytic capabilities have, in some instances, caused firms to push the role of human judgment and experience into the background. This is unfortunate, as the human factor is an essential part of the risk process and must not be overlooked or ignored. Professionals who have experienced first-hand problems, difficulties and losses caused by financial dislocations can bring their experience to bear in the daily management of risk. For instance, if, during a crisis event, a risk management model suggests that the wisest course of action is to hedge a trading book with US government securities, but a risk manager's own experiences during a similar historical event suggest that a swap hedge might be more effective, there is considerable wisdom in deferring to the experiences of the risk manager. Alternatively, if a model suggests that 10% overcollateralization is required to cover exposure but a risk officer suggests 20% is more appropriate during times of financial stress, deferring to human experience may be a wise course of action. This does not mean managing to "crisis standards" at all times — it simply means drawing on relevant experience and judgment when necessary. Naturally, there are times when experience and model recommendation coincide. However, when there is a divergence in views or recommendations, an institution must be prepared to support the wealth of human experience that exists in its management and control groups.

Human judgment and experience are so vital to risk management that this becomes one of the "cardinal rules."

3.6 INDEPENDENCE OF THE RISK FUNCTION MUST BE UNDOUBTED

The risk management function of a firm must be independent, with no reporting lines or responsibilities to those generating risks. When the risk function is not independent it cannot discharge its primary responsibility — protecting shareholders — without a conflict of interest. In Chapter 1 we cited the case of LTCM, the hedge fund controlled by Meriwether and a select group of partners. One of the apparent reasons for the fund's difficulties was lack of independent risk monitoring and enforcement; the partners that created and traded the strategies were the same partners responsible for overseeing risk positions and assigning capital to support strategies — there was no division between the two. While a risk committee met weekly to review the portfolio, it was not a forum where an independent risk officer could limit, critique or call into question the growing size of the risk positions; it was a forum for debating new strategies, markets, the amount of leverage to employ, and so forth. The presence of an independent risk function, accountable only to the head of LTCM and vested with sufficient authority to limit the fund's risks, might have produced a different outcome.

The governance structure created to define, monitor and manage the firm's overall risk profile must ensure that the unit responsible for allocating risk limits and making risk-related decisions has no reporting or compensation accountability to trading desks or business units. The senior risk officer of the firm must not have a reporting line to any senior business manager; the function should report through the chief financial office, or directly to the president or chief executive officer, with additional accountability to the risk committee. This ensures there can be no conflict of interest. Under no circumstances can risk officers be placed in situations where they might be compromised. For instance, if a portion of a risk officer's compensation is based on year-end reviews from senior trading managers, the risk officer may not be independent. It is not hard to conceive of a situation where the risk officer, eager for a handsome bonus, attempts to achieve good performance ratings from trading managers by agreeing to grant their risk requests.

The importance of creating, and maintaining, a separation between independent risk managers and risk takers is so fundamental to proper governance that it forms one of the "cardinal rules."

3.7 OTHER KEY CONTROL FUNCTIONS MUST REMAIN EQUALLY INDEPENDENT OF THE BUSINESS

In order to ensure the integrity of the overall control structure, other control units must remain independent of the business functions as well. Thus, legal, financial and operational officers must be under the direct management and supervision of those outside the business lines and their duties must not be influenced by business personnel. Failure to separate such control functions will, as noted earlier, lead to risk management problems, financial losses and possible bankruptcy. In the Barings case Leeson, as head of arbitrage trading and settlements, was able to trade, sign checks, confirm trades and reconcile exchange and bank statements — effectively controlling all front- and back-office duties; by doing so, he was able to assume any outright risk position desired, with little chance of being caught. Similar "lack of segregation" occurred at Sumitomo Corporation and Daiwa Bank — in both cases large financial losses followed.

3.8 THE RISK PROCESS MUST BE DYNAMIC IN ORDER TO BE TRULY EFFECTIVE

The truly effective risk process continuously reinvents itself. This should not be surprising, since the very nature of what a risk process attempts to control is dynamic — the financial markets, institutional participants, products and risk strategies that underpin every risk exposure are in a constant state of change. Failure to adapt to changing circumstances can lead to a rigid process and may heighten the likelihood of losses. The financial industry has recognized that continuously enhancing the risk process is a necessity. For instance, when credit risk concerns moved to the forefront during the LDC crisis of the 1980s, greater risk resources were committed to credit and lending procedures, reserves and capital. As the derivative debacles of the mid-1990s unfolded, more emphasis was placed on market risk measurement tools, derivative exposure methodologies and client suitability considerations. In the aftermath of the Russian and LTCM crises of 1998, the industry began uniting credit and market risk functions to ensure that leverage, liquidity/liquidation periods, collateral and correlated market/credit exposures were managed more effectively. The risk process has clearly been dynamic. While it is true that financial crises often spur changes, forward-thinking institutions implement enhancements well in advance of any problems, and are thus more likely to escape serious financial damage when crises do appear. Creating a dynamic risk process requires support of senior management and flexibility in the governance structure; it also demands risk personnel with a vision on how future market problems can be avoided.

3.9 DISCIPLINED APPLICATION OF THE RISK PROCESS IS A NECESSITY

The actual risk process created by a firm — governance, identification, quantification, reporting and ongoing management — must be applied with discipline throughout the organization, at all times. It is not acceptable to only enforce the process at certain times — this reduces its efficacy and erodes credibility. If a risk process is created to control risks, then it must be implemented and followed without fail, regardless of the circumstances. For instance, if risk limits are violated and those in the governance structure decide not to impose disciplinary action because the individual is considered a "star," then the risk process is not being applied consistently. In the same light, if a regular mechanism for verifying market prices for illiquid positions is suspended because a position under review is so large that it might cause a significant loss in the monthly income statement, then the risk process is not being followed as intended. Commitment to the development and implementation of a risk process means a commitment to applying directives at all times. Those in the governance structure, including directors, executives and risk committee members, must ensure disciplined application of risk rules.

3.10 AN INEFFECTIVE CONTROL PROCESS IS A SOURCE OF RISK THAT MUST BE ADDRESSED

A risk process that is ineffective in controlling risk is, itself, an incremental source of risk. A firm that believes its risk process is effective when it really is not derives a false sense of comfort that might lead it to do things it would not ordinarily do — such as assuming larger risks or expanding into new markets; this can lead to potentially severe consequences. As indicated in Chapter 1, a risk process may prove ineffective for a variety of reasons: senior management may not be an active participant in, or supporter of, risk management, meaning the function has little authority; the governance structure may be flawed, with directors, senior executive managers or risk committee members shirking responsibilities; the staff of the independent risk function may be comprised of relatively junior and inexperienced professionals who are not fully capable of dealing with the intricacies the discipline demands; violators of risk policies and limits may go unpunished; risk models and analytics may be overly naïve (or flawed) and of limited value in managing risk; and so forth. There are, of course, many other reasons why a risk process might be ineffective in controlling a firm's risks.

Determining whether a process is flawed is not easy, and can often be confirmed only after going through a market dislocation or period of financial volatility. Such episodes tend to produce losses; to the extent the losses are unexpected — in terms of source or magnitude — a firm may be able to locate the problem and formulate a solution. For instance, if, after a bout of market volatility across a wide range of asset classes, a firm finds that it has lost 10 times more than its VAR model suggested, it may have uncovered a problem in its VAR assumptions — perhaps the correlation assumptions are wrong, the liquidation period too short, or the confidence level too low. Knowing this, and wanting to take advantage of an "expensive" lesson, it may correct its risk process by using more conservative VAR parameters or employing additional portfolio risk measures that capture extreme events. Or, a firm that is active in the high yield bond market may sustain large losses after a series of high yield bond defaults; such losses may surprise executive management and the board of directors. In this case the firm may have experienced various risk process lapses: the risk function might have misinterpreted the board's mandate and granted limits that were more liberal than intended; alternatively, the risk function may have interpreted the mandate appropriately, but those in the governance structure may not have understood the magnitude of potential losses that could occur in the event of a dislocation. Prompt action must always be taken to cure any known or perceived problem in the risk control process.

3.11 RISK TAKERS MUST HAVE CLEAR REPORTING LINES AND ACCOUNTABILITIES

While all employees need to have clear reporting lines and accountability into the firm's management structure, a strong and direct management link is especially critical for those who are permitted to risk the firm's capital. There can be absolutely no ambiguity about a risk taker's management chain of command. The risk taker holds a very sensitive and critical position, in being responsible for the diligent allocation and management of scarce financial resources; he or she is in a position to make or lose a great deal of money for the firm and can do so almost instantaneously. The individual who occupies that position must, therefore, be managed and supervised properly. The risk taker must know to whom he or she is accountable and on what basis; equally, the manager must know that he or she is responsible for the activities of the risk taker. In a large and complex organization, with regional offices and product/division splits, a matrix of reporting lines might exist. In such instances it is even more important for all parties to be aware of management responsibilities. Where possible, joint reporting roles should be minimized — these can create management ambiguity, as each manager might assume the other is tending to personnel matters. Indeed, such was the case in the Leeson/Barings failure; Leeson had management accountability on both a regional basis (into Singapore) and a product basis (into the London-based financial products group) — neither provided the correct oversight of Leeson's activities, a contributing factor in the eventual demise of Barings. Ultimately, reporting clarity helps ensure proper communication of critical information and delegation of decision-making authorities. Firms that actively assume risk outside of a head office must have strong regional/local supervision. Certain dramatic failures of the risk process have occurred in satellite offices or regional subsidiaries (e.g. Barings/Singapore, Allfirst/Baltimore, Daiwa Bank/New York, and so on), suggesting that regional management must actively oversee the activities of regional risk takers.

3.12 COMPENSATION POLICIES FOR RISK TAKERS MUST BE RATIONAL

Many individuals enter the world of risk-taking and business origination in order to earn as much money as possible — for their firms and, ultimately, for themselves. While this is an admirable goal, it is also one that must be kept in check. "Incorrect" incentives can skew an individual's behavior and might ultimately lead to control problems. For instance, if a trader is paid a percentage of all profits generated for the firm, he or she might be inclined to assume large, or unwise, risks — to the potential detriment of the firm. If a trader takes a great deal of risk and makes a large amount of money, he or she will receive a large bonus and continue on for another year. If a trader takes significant risks but has a poor year, he or she will receive a poor bonus (or none at all), may decide future opportunities at the firm are bleak, and depart. This leaves the firm without a risk taker and, potentially, with a large amount of risk that needs to be managed. In the same light, a compensation policy that allows a trader to "present value" the financial gains of long-term deals with "tail risk" may skew the firm's risk profile towards illiquid, long-dated risk. For instance, knowing that a 20-year swap will generate more profit than a one-year swap, and knowing that the present value of the deal will be used to compute bonuses, a trader may book as many 20-year swaps as possible. The company may thus be left with a great deal of illiquid, and possibly unhedgeable, long-term risk. A compensation policy that provides for correct incentives, without encouraging dangerous behavior, is ideal. Ultimately, the economic incentives given to risk takers and their managers should be aligned with the firm's long-term financial performance; this is the best way to avoid problematic behavior.

3.13 TRADING MANAGERS AND INVESTMENT BANKERS SHOULD BE THE FRONT LINE OF RISK MANAGEMENT — ACCOUNTABLE, IN A MEASURABLE WAY, FOR ASSUMING "GOOD" RISKS

Independent risk officers often think of themselves as the managers of a firm's risk. In a sense, they are — they provide an independent assessment of risk and are typically given sufficient flexibility within the governance structure to shape aspects of a firm's risk profile. But the true managers of a firm's risk are the business originators and trading managers that build relationships, source trades, create structures and underwrite deals. These professionals are paid to generate revenues, and generally do so through risky businesses (exceptions might center on transactions such as advisory assignments, best-efforts capital market placements, and so on). As such, traders and bankers should be regarded as the true managers of a firm's risk capital. In that role, they should be responsible for making sure the risk that they assume is appropriate for the firm — that is, priced correctly and accommodated within the profile and capacity parameters defined by the risk committee and the board of directors; they should also be responsible for managing risks on an ongoing basis. Though client imperatives and demands sometimes place traders and bankers in the awkward position of having to assume risk that may not be optimal, they must be discouraged from doing so through an objective mechanism (e.g. a risk-adjusted return framework). If front-line risk managers put "good" risk on the books, the entire firm benefits; as such, they must be given the right tools for doing so and must be compensated in an appropriate fashion. Independent risk managers remain a vital link in the process, of course, and any view to the contrary will almost certainly result in a flawed governance mechanism. But risk managers are generally not intended to be the "first line of defense" — business revenue generators are responsible for balancing risk and reward to obtain the best possible outcome from the firm.

3.14 ONCE MANAGEMENT HAS CONFIDENCE IN ITS RISK PROCESS, IT SHOULD LET BUSINESS MANAGERS CONDUCT BUSINESS AND MONITOR THE RESULTS

Senior management responsible for risk is typically not interested in micro-managing risk processes by becoming actively involved in the minutiae of individual deals, trades and transactions. The same is generally true for the credit and market risk officers charged with daily oversight of particular business units or counterparty relationships; while most take an interest in the direction of the business and events that might impact risk profiles, they are unlikely to be involved in the particulars of each deal, trade ticket or termsheet. If a company has confidence in its risk process (as it should, if it has created an effective governance framework that controls all known risks) then it must simply let the process function as intended. As indicated, business managers, not risk officers, are the first line of defense in the daily management of risks. Only when there is a potential issue, problem or opportunity should risk officers assume a more active role; at any other time they are more likely to be a hindrance than a help. In addition to operating more efficiently firms that allow the risk process to work as intended send a strong message to investors and regulators regarding the strength of their control process.

3.15 APPROPRIATE LIMITS SHOULD EXIST TO CONTROL RISKS

Risk limits are generally used to numerically define a firm's risk appetite and effectively constrain the amount of risk that can be taken or granted in specific markets, assets or credits. Though they are only one tool in the arsenal of the independent risk function, they are perhaps the most useful, and tangible, mechanism for controlling risk. Limits also provide a common communication link between risk officers and business managers. While a business manager might not understand (or even care about) issues such as corporate cash flow, leverage or capitalization — which are of considerable importance to the credit officer — he or she will certainly understand, and care about, the amount of credit risk that can be accommodated under risk limits; the same applies with market risks and associated limits.

A suite of risk limits that properly constrains all risks that have been identified is a necessary dimension of effective risk management. Limits must be constructed and applied in a way that corrals all exposures; failure to limit a significant exposure can lead to potential losses. A balance, however, must be struck. At a certain point, a matrix of limits that seeks to constrain risk in combinations that are unlikely to occur can be counterproductive — a great deal of time may be spent trying to compute exposures and interpret risk limit matrices that may serve no practical purpose. It is far more useful for a risk officer to create limits that control the critical risk dimensions of a business. Indeed, risk limits should exist to control the exposures of a specific business; since individual desks may have very different risk measures, it is likely that some aggregation of risk limits will be required at higher levels within the governance structure. Aggregate limits may thus be developed for the entire firm and then subdivided to individual businesses on a customized basis (e.g. a "top down" approach), or individual limits may be developed on a business-specific basis and aggregated to produce a firm-wide total (e.g. a "bottom up" approach). For instance, a European bond desk will be exposed to European credit spreads and its Japanese and US counterparts to their own local credit spreads; each should thus be constrained through specific risk limits. Such control granularity is unlikely to be necessary at the level of the risk committee or board of directors; accordingly, an overall credit spread risk limit might be established (e.g. total loss for a specified move in any global credit spread). Striking the right balance of limits is a critical part of the risk management process; risk officers should resist imposing too many limits, which creates a tedious and unworkable process, but must not impose too few limits, which might allow risks to go unmanaged.

3.16 RISK POLICIES SHOULD BE USED TO DEFINE AND CONTROL ALL RISK ACTIVITIES

Risk policies that define a firm's risk-taking activities should be created by the independent risk function, approved by the risk committee and sanctioned by the board. Risk policies are typically designed to express what can, and cannot, be done in individual risk-taking businesses and products. In order for business leaders to understand the constraints placed on their operations, they must be able to refer to a policy document which outlines, as succinctly as possible, the control parameters of the business. Risk policies must cover any business activity that generates risk; failure to apply a risk policy when required could lead to unexpected losses. Policies should be as clear, and unambiguous, as possible; under no circumstances should they be subject to "interpretation." This leads to confusion, debate and conflict, as those trying to interpret the "letter versus the spirit" of the policy may actually commit the firm to risks it was not prepared to take; crafting a clear policy reduces the chance of misinterpretation. Care must also be taken to ensure risk policies are consistent with the firm's risk mandate; the policy documents should not permit businesses to operate outside of the specific risk mandate conveyed by the board of directors and risk committee. In addition, businesses carrying similar risks must be treated in the same fashion (unless there is a specific reason not to); failure to do so may lead to internal "arbitrage" and a possible breakdown in process.

3.17 A NEW PRODUCT PROCESS SHOULD EXIST TO EVALUATE THE NUANCES AND COMPLEXITIES OF NEW INSTRUMENTS, MARKETS AND TRANSACTIONS; THE SAME SHOULD APPLY TO CAPITAL COMMITMENTS

The establishment of mechanisms that can be used to vet new products, structures and capital commitments is an important component of the risk governance structure. Such committees must be independent of the business functions; while they are likely to feature business representation, they should be steered by independent control professionals under authorities granted by the risk committee and board of directors. Though such mechanisms can assume different forms, the basic premise is to provide a forum for analyzing, reviewing and discussing ventures that are new to the firm — including new products, deals or business lines. By creating and using such committees, business sponsors can join with control personnel (which may include risk professionals, as well as their colleagues from finance, legal, operations, audit and technology) in analyzing and understanding the risks posed by new instruments or businesses. For instance, if a firm is contemplating local fixed income trading through a Latin American office, a new product committee can help verify that all control issues and procedures are properly developed, discussed and agreed before proceeding. Since the proposal might generate unique and important control issues, a forum for discussion and analysis is essential in order to protect the interests of the firm. When the process is working effectively, such a forum permits open discussion, challenge and debate; when it is not, it becomes a "rubber stamp" exercise, where all proposals put forth by business unit sponsors are approved without question. Accordingly, committees must be guided by independent control officers who are senior and experienced. Participants should be empowered to make decisions on behalf of their functions; staffing new product committees with junior members does not guarantee that the right questions will be asked or that business leaders will be challenged — experience is an essential ingredient in the process. Capital commitment committees, created to review terms of very large capital transactions (e.g. block equity trades, bought deals, firm underwritings, and so on), are likely to be comprised of market and credit risk officers, legal officers and business personnel. Since many deals are time-sensitive (in contrast to new product/business development, which may have a life cycle spanning weeks or months), capital commitment committees must be prepared to meet on short-notice and arrive at decisions quickly; once again, senior personnel must drive the process in order to ensure that thorough discussion and analysis occur before decisions are taken. Similar committees might be established to review client suitability issues, reserves, and so forth. To ensure the efficacy of new product and commitment committees, it is helpful for the risk committee and board of directors to receive regular updates regarding the outcome of any decisions that have been taken; this establishes strong upward communication and allows risk committee members and directors to be aware of significant new endeavors that might impact the firm's risk profile.

3.18 THE NATURE AND STRUCTURE OF RISK POLICIES, METRICS AND REPORTING SHOULD BE REVIEWED REGULARLY TO ACCOUNT FOR CHANGING DIMENSIONS OF BUSINESS

Financial markets are dynamic and the institutions, participants, products, deals and regulations that comprise the market change on a continuous basis; this means credit, market and other risks are in a constant state of change as well. A risk process that is relevant at a given point in time may be less relevant as the environment begins to shift — it must therefore be flexible and adaptable, able to change as needed. A rigid process that has to be "reinvented" whenever new products or business lines are added, or when credit or trading conventions or regulations change, hinders the effective management of risk and may ultimately collapse. From a practical perspective, the independent risk management function may engage in regular annual reviews of the firm's risk policies, risk limit allocation process and quantification methodologies; this can take place more frequently if warranted. When undertaking policy reviews, proposed changes should be discussed with business unit managers, since they are likely to be impacted by any changes. The risk committee and the board of directors should be advised of, and sanction, all proposed enhancements — this helps ensure that all responsible parties are aware of, and can be held accountable for, any changes. For instance, a firm active in extending credit through derivative transactions is likely to feature a series of policies that describe future credit exposure methodologies. As computing and analytic techniques improve, new derivative products are introduced and underlying derivative reference data is strengthened, the risk function should revisit its approach to quantifying credit exposures. As a result of changes in the marketplace it may want to update and enhance its quantitative methodologies and risk policies; after consulting with business leaders and completing enhancements, the risk function should advise others in the business and governance structure. Similar reviews of other businesses may yield risk policy/process enhancements of their own.

3.19 AN EFFECTIVE DISCIPLINARY SYSTEM IS CRUCIAL; IF LIMITS/POLICIES ARE BREACHED, QUICK DISCIPLINARY ACTION MUST BE TAKEN — IF DECISIVE ACTION IS NOT TAKEN, THE RISK GOVERNANCE PROCESS LOSES CREDIBILITY

Risk processes exist in order to protect the firm and its shareholders from losing too much money. As noted earlier, a key element of the process is the establishment of risk limits and risk/new product committees to cap and control the type/amount of risk exposure facing a firm. The effective risk process can tolerate no violations of controls (whether policies, limits or the rules of risk/new product forums). Violations, whether willful or accidental, must be handled decisively. Disciplinary action can vary, and may depend on the type of infraction that has occurred. For instance, a flagrant disregard of risk limits/policies may be grounds for dismissal while a breach of limits or policies due to market moves or simple error may be dealt with through warning letters or financial penalties. Failure to penalize a risk violation can cause at least two problems: internal disregard for the risk process, which might lead to damaging consequences if left unchecked; and a risk function with little, or no, credibility in the eyes of business managers, directors and regulators. Both problems are potentially dangerous. If business managers believe they can flout risk directives without penalty, they may take bigger bets with the firm's capital; this may ultimately lead to large financial losses. Risk managers who are ineffective in disciplining those who violate rules and regulations will be questioned by others in the governance structure and regulatory community; this might lead to criticism of the function and may reflect more broadly on the firm's entire control structure.

Care must be taken to apply disciplinary actions consistently. Ineffective application of discipline can occur when a significant business producer violates a risk policy or limit. If the individual generates considerable income for the firm, a "double standard" might be applied — disciplining the individual in some minor form, but ensuring that his or her career is not damaged. While an average performer might be dismissed in the event of a violation, the same may not occur when it involves a "star." Such a double standard is clearly unacceptable. The severity or leniency of a penalty should not be related to revenues, skills or seniority — equal treatment should be applied to anyone who violates the risk process. It is also important to establish violation procedures for all risk-sensitive areas — not just credit and market risks, but any area that generates a risk exposure. For instance, if a firm has an unsigned legal document backlog (e.g. master swap agreements or credit agreements) it runs a certain amount of operational and legal risk exposure. In the extreme, a default when documents are not in order might lead to financial losses. Inaction by business units in resolving documentary backlogs should be viewed as an infraction of policy and penalized in a predefined fashion.

3.20 THE RISK ORGANIZATION MUST CARRY STATURE, EXPERIENCE AND AUTHORITY IN ORDER TO COMMAND RESPECT

The risk management function tends to be highly visible within corporate, and particularly financial, organizations — this has become particularly true over the past few years as financial crises have brought considerable focus to risk management practices. Since risk functions are in the limelight, there is considerable logic and benefit to staffing the team with experienced professionals who are empowered to implement and manage the process. Spending incremental resources to attract the very best risk professionals is often an effective strategy. Experienced individuals possess the knowledge, maturity and stature needed to manage the function properly; since risk officers in large organizations are typically granted considerable decision-making authority, a firm must consider hiring experienced professionals. Firms that relegate risk management to the "back-office," or structure it as an administrative risk reporting function with no real decision-making authority, miss an opportunity to define and implement a strong risk culture. While not every firm has the luxury of staffing their risk function with the best available talent, those able to do so make an explicit statement about the value of risk control within the corporate organization. This brings benefits to management and employees, and can strengthen dealings with regulators, auditors and shareholders. By spending time and effort to create a risk organization with stature, a firm is investing in its long-term financial goals.

3.21 THE KNOWLEDGE THAT AN EXPERIENCED GROUP OF PROFESSIONALS IS SCRUTINIZING RISK IS A VERY POWERFUL RISK MANAGEMENT TOOL

Continuing with the rule above, when traders, bankers, marketers or originators are aware that risk-bearing businesses are being scrutinized by teams of skilled professionals, they often pay closer attention to the process. If an institution structures its risk management function as an administrative unit, risk takers may not believe that exposures are being properly reviewed or that value is being added; it is possible, under this scenario, that the process will not be taken as seriously as it should. In contrast, when the function is considered to be knowledgeable and experienced, a greater sense of risk awareness develops. For example, a 20-year trading veteran who acts as a firm's senior risk officer is likely to be able to command the time, attention and respect of senior trading managers and business leaders; business managers will come to know and value the experience the senior risk officer brings to bear, and should find his or her input an important part of the business process. If similar high-caliber professionals form the core of the risk function, business managers are likely to be more attentive.

3.22 HIRING THE BEST RISK EXPERTS AVAILABLE, WITH A BROAD RANGE OF CREDIT, MARKET, LEGAL AND QUANTITATIVE EXPERIENCE, IS A WORTHWHILE INVESTMENT IN THE FIRM'S FUTURE

Expanding on the theme above, there are generally two different approaches to the creation of an independent risk function. The first model calls for creation of a risk administration unit staffed by junior to mid-level professionals with a solid understanding of, and a certain amount of experience in, risk analysis and reporting issues. This is a workable approach, though one with limitations — it is effectively an administration, rather than management, function, as reporting and analysis, rather than management of risk, tends to be the focus. The second model centers on the creation of a true "management" function with duties that include monitoring, reporting and managing. Management involves difficult decision-making and demands the skills and experience of seasoned professionals; some of these professionals may have served in business or line functions, and may thus be very conversant with different aspects of business development and profit management. This approach, while more expensive, signals management's support for a risk function that is capable of actively managing the firm's risk, not simply reporting and analyzing it. Given the frequency and severity of financial crises that occurred during the 1990s and into the early part of the 21st century, it has become increasingly common for institutions to allocate resources to the development of risk functions that are staffed by professionals capable of active and diligent management of risk; most recognize that the cost/benefit trade-off is well worthwhile.

3.23 ENSURING THE RISK FUNCTION POSSESSES THE RIGHT MIX OF SKILLS AND EXPERIENCE STRENGTHENS THE MANAGEMENT PROCESS

A firm creating a risk function should ensure it features the right combination of professional skills. For instance, though credit and market risk share common ground, they are fundamentally different disciplines with unique perspectives and approaches; accordingly, talents from both groups are necessary in order to create a proper risk function. Market risk professionals tend to be "market-savvy," sensitive to changing market conditions, and good at developing quick solutions; since many market risk managers are ex-risk takers, they have a very keen appreciation of pricing, hedging and liquidity matters. Credit risk professionals, in contrast, often come from commercial banking and rating agency backgrounds. Many are very analytical and often excel at dissecting financial statements/structures and reviewing loan documentation and covenants. The skills of market and credit professionals are complimentary to the total corporate risk management organization, and both should be added. The same applies to other areas where risks need to be managed — legal, operations/settlement, audit, financial control, and so forth. Each area is characterized by specific knowledge that can be utilized to create a stronger management process.

3.24 RISK TAKERS, RISK MANAGERS AND OTHER CONTROL PROFESSIONALS SHOULD ROTATE REGULARLY TO REMAIN "FRESH" IN THEIR EXPERIENCE AND PERSPECTIVES

Risk takers, risk managers and other high-level control professionals work in high-pressure jobs where they carry a great deal of responsibility and authority; the financial fortunes of the firms they work for are often at stake based on the quality and precision of the work they perform. While gaining the experience to perform these duties takes years to achieve — making a firm loathe to transfer or rotate them into new functions — it is vital for these professionals to remain energized and motivated. It is often wise for management to rotate or promote talented individuals into other positions within the firm, and bring new talent into the positions they vacate. This does not mean that every producer and risk professional should be replaced on a set schedule, or that profitable business or strong control discipline should be disrupted — such would be counterproductive. It does suggest, however, that there are times and opportunities for enhancing the value of the employee's career and outlook by broadening horizons and removing some of the pressures associated with revenue generation and risk management. The process also gives younger professionals the opportunity to move into similar roles and expand the firm's overall skills. It is important for those in very intense positions to remain as "fresh" as possible in their views and perspectives; as in any discipline, remaining in one role for too long can lead to a loss of acuity, energy and response time. When this occurs, more significant problems may arise — including errors, mistakes in judgment, and so on. The firm benefits on all fronts when it is able to institute a regular program of rotation and promotion.

3.25 RISK EXPERTISE MUST BE DISSEMINATED THROUGHOUT THE ORGANIZATION

A company that actively assumes risk must ensure that the skills needed to manage risk (from both a front-office and control perspective) are disseminated throughout the organization. It is imperative that knowledge of risk exposures, and techniques for managing such exposures, not reside exclusively with a very small cadre of experts. Though a firm may have exceptionally talented business leaders responsible for a significant amount of revenues and risks, it must not expose itself to "key man risk" — the risk that the departure of a single business leader, or a small group of experts, with significant business and risk knowledge will cause business disruptions or broader risk management problems. For instance, a bond-trading boutique may take significant risk in the high yield markets, and be exceptionally profitable in doing so, through the efforts of half a dozen individuals. These professionals may have an excellent understanding of the market, its risk dynamics, hedging strategies, valuations, and so forth. However, that knowledge may reside exclusively within the small group. Senior managers, junior traders, risk managers and controllers may lack detailed knowledge on how the team takes and manages its risk. If the bond team leaves, the firm instantly loses its market presence, knowledge, profitability and, most importantly, risk management skills; exiting the market (particularly one that may be characterized by illiquidity) might expose the firm to considerable risk of loss. Accordingly, a regular practice of disseminating risk expertise to other senior managers, business leaders and risk officers — through rotations, detailed discussions, risk updates, and so on — should be part of the governance process. This minimizes the chance that key man risk will impact the firm and makes the entire firm a more prudent and experienced manager of businesses and risks.

3.26 PRESERVING AN INSTITUTIONAL MEMORY OF RISK ISSUES IS IMPORTANT FOR FUTURE MANAGEMENT OF RISK WITHIN A COMPANY

Though every large organization is exposed to personnel turnover — either within or outside the firm — it is important to create a mechanism that allows the memory of institutional risk management to be preserved; this allows a firm to continually expand its core knowledge base. Different mechanisms can be used to preserve an institutional memory: requiring senior managers within the firm's top management committee to be involved with risk issues on an ongoing basis (e.g. by becoming participants in the risk governance process); documenting in detail how different risk structures have evolved, how different financial crises have impacted risk-bearing operations and what lessons have been learned during market dislocations, and making such material part of the ongoing risk education process; rotating key trading managers through the risk management function so that they develop, and disseminate, an understanding of the risk function; permitting risk managers to rotate through different parts of the organization so that they can impart risk knowledge to a broader audience; and so forth. Any device that preserves risk memory will help build a stronger risk culture.

3.27 GENERAL RISK EDUCATION SHOULD BE MANDATORY THROUGHOUT THE FIRM

Educating staff about risk management matters is an important practice that generates greater risk awareness throughout the firm. Education should, however, be tailored to the needs of specific audiences; for instance, the requirements of executive management are likely to be quite different than those of desk-level controllers and auditors. Senior managers might need education on "high level" risk measures and issues, while those dealing with individual traders and businesses might need to focus on detailed risk measures and techniques. Senior management may not understand risk in the same way as business managers, traders and bankers, and should be educated to the point where they are comfortable and conversant with major risk issues. While senior managers may have an appreciation of business issues, they may not all understand different dimensions of risk; it is unrealistic to believe that traders and bankers, who deal with risk on a daily basis, think about the risk discipline in the same fashion as the senior managers who are devoted to guiding the tactical and strategic direction of the firm. Though senior managers may not have the same grasp of the topic, they are often called on to make difficult risk decisions or discuss the firm's risk profile with external parties. Accordingly, a sequence of "executive risk education," which covers the fundamentals of risk-taking and risk management, is advisable. This helps senior managers discharge their fiduciary responsibilities with greater confidence and permits traders and bankers to ensure risk-related issues are understood at the highest levels of the firm. More detailed general education related to the analysis and interpretation of risk should be extended to others in the firm. Teaching managers and staff members in the finance, treasury, audit, operations and legal departments about risk ensures a greater understanding of the process; over the medium-term these staff members may gain enough knowledge to advise risk officers about important risk issues they uncover. As in any educational endeavor, it is important to update the process regularly.

3.28 EDUCATIONAL EFFORTS SHOULD FOCUS ON CONCEPTS THAT ARE PART OF THE DAILY OPERATING ENVIRONMENT

Extending the rule above, the education process should incorporate terms and concepts that have become part of the financial mainstream. Though some concepts are mathematically complex, they can often be simplified and used by a broader audience. An educational exercise related to measures such as VAR, future exposure, stress testing, and so on is likely to be worthwhile, since these concepts are widely used and discussed at all levels in a firm. They are also referenced by outside parties, including regulators, equity analysts, shareholders and rating agency analysts. For instance, senior managers must possess basic knowledge of what VAR means and conveys. It does not mean that they need to be experts on the subject, or even understand the intricacies of which methodology is being employed — that is best left to experts in the risk and trading functions. However, being conversant with the topic helps ensure mutual understanding of key risk parameters and comfort and confidence when communicating with external parties.

3.29 RISK SPECIALISTS SHOULD QUESTION AND PROBE UNTIL THEY ARE SATISFIED WITH THE ANSWERS — THEY SHOULD NOT BE AFRAID TO QUERY AND CHALLENGE "BUSINESS EXPERTS," EVEN WHEN IT SEEMS DIFFICULT TO DO SO

We have indicated that risk is a broad and complex topic. It spans a variety of disciplines — credit, market, operational, legal, and so on — each with its own nuances and body of "required knowledge." It is not possible for even the most astute risk managers to have an in-depth command of all aspects of the subject; specialists are, therefore, essential. Those who focus on specific sectors, industries, assets and markets can bring their skills to bear in identifying, understanding, monitoring and managing risk. Sufficient resources should be devoted to the risk effort to ensure that specializations are possible. For example, there is little point in assigning responsibility for high-grade industrial credit exposures to an equity risk manager — the disciplines, and required skills, are entirely different. Once a cadre of risk specialists has been established, they must probe all relevant risk management matters in their jurisdictions. While there is often a "fear" of appearing ignorant in front of business experts sponsoring a risk-bearing deal or business, there is simply no question, issue or topic that should not be raised and explored. Risk specialists must always analyze all risk-related issues thoroughly; indeed, they have a fiduciary responsibility to do so. It is worth noting that business experts are not infallible in their knowledge and may not always know as much as they should — business managers can often learn from specialist risk managers.

3.30 RISK MANAGEMENT SPANS MANY FRONTS — ALLIES IN AUDIT, FINANCE, LEGAL AND OPERATIONS CAN HELP IN THE PROCESS

An effective risk governance structure centers heavily on communication and cooperation. Most firms feature multiple control organizations, departments and mechanisms that create and maintain a control environment. While each specialty area has its own focus — for instance, controllers are likely to be interested in valuations, P&L, and books and records, legal specialists in guarantees, confirmations, master agreements, and so on — all are fundamentally interested in creating a proper framework of controls. Making sure that each of these departments is in regular communication with the others is an important element of governance. For example, auditors, controllers, lawyers and risk officers often encounter similar issues/concerns when considering risk-bearing business or transactions. Though each may view the risk or control issue from a unique angle, the ability to coordinate and share information can be very valuable. Channels that create lines of communication across different control functions should be developed to encourage regular dialog. In the broadest application of this concept, rotation of control professionals through different groups can deepen knowledge and strengthen ties.

3.31 A CONSTRUCTIVE RELATIONSHIP WITH BUSINESS UNITS CAN BE MORE PRODUCTIVE THAN AN ADVERSARIAL ONE; BUT A CONSTRUCTIVE RELATIONSHIP DOES NOT MEAN APPROVING ALL BUSINESS DEALS AND RISKS

Risk officers and business managers can benefit from regular communication and cooperation — a productive relationship between the two groups ultimately creates a stronger risk control framework. Business managers must come to understand that, in a properly functioning institution, risk officers are to be regarded as allies, not adversaries. Though some organizations preserve, and sometimes promote, differences between control personnel and business producers, enlightened organizations have come to realize that educated and market-sensitive risk officers can help a business by preventing problems when risks appear unwise, and acting as supporters when risks appear wise. When a constructive relationship exists between the two functions, information and solicitation of opinions tends to be forthcoming; strong two-way communication follows, and a more efficient risk management process develops. In contrast, when relationships are adversarial — perhaps risk officers are not perceived as knowledgeable or value-added by their business counterparts or business leaders fail to give risk managers the attention they deserve — friction develops and communication falters. Once this happens, risk managers may be prone to overreacting and making incorrect decisions; this is of little benefit to the control or business functions, or the institution at large. A constructive relationship is, therefore, a far more workable and beneficial solution. That said, a constructive relationship does not mean that the risk function should approve all requests for risk capacity. A business unit that takes advantage of a positive relationship with an independent risk manager by persuading the risk manager to allow it to assume unwise risk is acting against the interests and principles of the firm; any risk officer that succumbs to such influence should, at a minimum, be removed from a decision-making role. The experienced risk professional knows how to manage relationships so that communication between risk and business officers is constructive even when risks are rejected or restructured.

3.32 RISK DECISIONS SHOULD BE MADE QUICKLY AND FIRMLY; OVERRULING THE DECISIONS OF RISK SUBORDINATES SHOULD BE KEPT TO AN ABSOLUTE MINIMUM

Global capital flows and instant information cause financial markets to move with incredible speed. Accordingly, many risk decisions have to be made in relatively short time frames. While it is true that larger, structured transactions often feature enough lead time to be considered and analyzed at a somewhat slower pace, many deals require quick analysis and decision-making. Failure to create a process that can address "short fuse" decisions may result in the loss of business to competitors. In addition to being able to respond quickly, decisions must be firm and clear. Any action by a risk officer that is open to interpretation can result in lost business or assumption of ill-advised risk. Thus, if a trader requests a credit officer to provide an approval for a particular transaction with a counterparty, the credit officer should, under normal circumstances, be able to communicate an answer quickly and decisively.

Management of the "risk decision hierarchy" is also critical. During times of high pressure, when a trader or banker receives a negative answer from a risk officer, there may be a tendency to elevate or "appeal" the decision to higher management levels — in hopes of a reversal (i.e. a favorable response). When managers routinely overturn the decisions of subordinates, communication and credibility between business units and risk officers is likely to be undermined. Traders and bankers, knowing that a more positive response might be obtained from senior risk officials, might circumvent "lower levels" by referring all issues to senior management. This creates dissatisfaction at all levels within the risk organization, and is indicative of a flawed governance structure. It is imperative that senior management support the decision-making of subordinates unless there is a significant error in the interpretation of information or risk policies; failure to provide support will quickly cause internal problems.

3.33 CONSISTENCY IS VITAL THROUGHOUT THE RISK CONTROL ORGANIZATION; THIS ELIMINATES THE POSSIBILITY OF "INTERNAL ARBITRAGE" ACROSS REGIONS AND BUSINESSES

Once a risk governance structure has been created, it is important for the governing risk authority to promulgate consistent rules and policies. These should be as clear and consistent as possible and leave no room for doubt or misinterpretation; failure to do so can result in "subjective" interpretation by different businesses and regions. Taken to its extreme, inconsistent standards (e.g. policies which treat identical risks in very different ways) can lead to "internal arbitrage;" this can create considerable problems and may ultimately cause a breakdown in the risk control process. For instance, if a risk policy governing the US interest rate derivative desk requires that collateral be taken on all trades with sub-investment grade counterparties, but the same requirement does not exist with the Euro interest rate desk, there exists considerable incentive for the US traders to book transactions through the Euro desk. In instances where consistent risk standards are not applicable differences, and the rationale for such differences, should be well publicized.

3.34 RISK OFFICERS SHOULD BE INVOLVED IN EVERY ASPECT OF THE FIRM THAT HAS A RISK DIMENSION TO ENSURE THAT THE PROPER PERSPECTIVE IS ALWAYS REPRESENTED

In order for a risk management process to be truly effective, those responsible for developing and managing the function need to be involved in every aspect of strategy, business or control development that impacts risk. Since knowledge of risk management and risk process is a relatively specialized discipline, those who are sufficiently experienced to make decisions that will affect a firm's risk control framework must participate actively in all relevant forums. For instance, when creating trading platforms risk representatives should play an active role, as most systems must feature credit and market risk functionality in order to be useful and effective; being part of the initial team that develops risk requirements helps ensure that no "surprises" appear in the future. The same is true for new developments related to legal, audit or finance processes, or to actual changes or enhancements in business strategy. The "risk voice" should be present whenever necessary.

3.35 A RISK CRISIS MANAGEMENT PROGRAM, WITH CLEAR AUTHORITIES, RESPONSIBILITIES AND EXPECTATIONS, SHOULD BE DESIGNED FOR QUICK IMPLEMENTATION

When a market crisis (or some other disruptive event) strikes it is important for a firm to be able to immediately activate a pre-established crisis management program with an appropriate "chain of command." This helps ensure that critical risk and funding tasks are prioritized, information is directed to the right parties and timely decisions are taken. It is virtually impossible to create an effective "emergency" risk process while a crisis is underway. Communication links are poor, misinformation characterizes most activities, and actions may be taken on the basis of erroneous facts. Accordingly, it is crucial to establish a crisis management process in advance of any dislocation; given the relative frequency of financial dislocations over the past two decades, this effectively means that a firm needs to establish a program as a priority. By creating a crisis program a firm's senior executives can quickly focus their attention on areas that might be impacted by market stress — accessing funding on an emergency basis, "liquefying" the balance sheet, neutralizing risk positions with proxy hedges, and so forth. By instituting a well-publicized "chain of command" risk officers, treasury officers and business unit managers know whom to contact, how to share information and how to escalate news and information so that risk and financial decisions can be made quickly. For instance, once a crisis is underway the chain of command might require junior risk mangers to elevate issues directly to the senior risk officer or chief financial officer; they, in turn, might have direct access to a subgroup of board members in order to advise on risk decisions or seek approval for exceptional circumstances. Senior business leaders might receive special dispensation to approve certain risk-related trades on a unilateral basis. Any crisis management program that temporarily circumvents established governance procedures must, of course, be well defined, codified and approved by the governance parties before being implemented. The process should also define when temporary crisis measures are no longer required and when business and control procedures are expected to return to normal.

3.36 SENSITIVITY TO REGULATORY REQUIREMENTS IS IMPORTANT

Regulators play an important role in the advancement of risk management processes and their directives and requirements must be taken seriously. Though firms may periodically feel "overwhelmed" by the number of rules and regulations that must be followed, or the quantity of risk information which must be submitted, they must remember that the requirements exist for a reason — to ensure that a firm has a prudent risk process or to help identify and resolve process problems. Though the regulatory process is not perfect, and certainly not guaranteed to solve every problem or forestall every disaster, the efforts are an important step forward in an environment where markets are increasingly volatile and interdependent. By ensuring that firms that fall under the jurisdiction of a particular regulatory authority adhere to established rules, the markets gain comfort and security that participants meet minimum financial and control standards. Far greater benefit can be gained when institutions operate through companies or subsidiaries subject to regulatory oversight — rather than offshore entities that may not be subject to the same rules. Greater transparency, of course, comes at a price — typically in the form of additional personnel and infrastructure to ensure that regulatory requirements are being addressed. This is generally regarded as a worthwhile investment, as is the occasional inconvenience of having to provide alternate forms of information. As indicated, the regulatory process is not perfect; just because regulators demand adherence to particular rules or insist on specific types of reporting does not mean that problems will be avoided. Many examples serve as reminders of "less than perfect" regulatory mechanisms, and reinforce the fact that regulations alone cannot act as a substitute for internal risk processes. Nonetheless, sensitivity to the demands of regulators is an important part of governance, and well worth the time and effort.

3.37 THE GOVERNANCE PROCESS MUST PROVIDE SENIOR MANAGERS WITH AN ABILITY TO VIEW AND MANAGE RISK ON A REGULATORY/LEGAL ENTITY BASIS

While individual book-runners and traders care primarily about the risk that they are responsible for managing, risk officers and business managers are generally interested in reviewing consolidated risk profiles that reflect the exposures a firm has across products and geographic regions. For instance, if a firm runs Japanese interest rate risk in London, New York and Tokyo, a shift in the market will affect the positions in each center and, by definition, the consolidated position — this is the firm's true exposure. While consolidated risk views across products and national boundaries are very useful from an overall corporate risk management perspective, the proper governance structure must also provide for risk views by legal entity. This is particularly important in an era where local regulators hold senior executives and directors of each individual legal entity accountable for the risk they run in their units. To ensure the governance process functions as intended, local legal entity risk must be visible to the local executives; they must also be given, in certain instances, authority to influence or reshape the local entity's risk profile. For instance, if a global firm operates a broad-based book of risk businesses, including currency and equity trading through an important London-based legal entity, it must be able to segregate all London risk exposures — including market and credit risks associated with the currency and equity businesses. The London directors can then claim to have access to risk information that permits discussion, analysis and possible management action. More importantly, directors will be able to discharge their fiduciary duties in an effective and prudent manner, and regulators will derive comfort from the fact that local managers and directors have sufficient information to manage the risk of the local legal entity.

3.38 REGULAR INTERNAL AUDITS OF THE RISK PROCESS SHOULD BE PERFORMED

In order to ensure that the risk governance structure in general, and the risk management process in particular, operates in an effective manner, regular audits should be performed by the firm's internal audit function. The audit program should be thorough enough to identify potential failures in risk process, communication, policy, enforcement, and so on. Large firms often have auditors dedicated to ongoing review of the risk function. Since the discipline is specialized, and since it covers a diverse group of areas (including credit risk, market risk, risk technology, quantitative risk, and so on), this is often an effective use of resources. When dedicated risk auditors are available, they can review individual components of the risk process; by the time they have completed their overall work they will be ready to commence the process again. Smaller firms that do not have the resources necessary to hire dedicated risk auditors may opt to conduct general external audits of the governance process; these can be supplemented by reviews of select "priority" areas. For example, if a firm has implemented a new risk technology platform that produces risk aggregation and reporting for management and regulators, a specific audit of the platform is advisable. Likewise, if special limits have been created to cap a specific type of risk, an audit of their efficacy in controlling risk exposure might be warranted.

Summarizing the simple rules applicable to the risk governance process, we note the following:

- The effective governance framework begins by defining the firm's risk philosophy in terms of risk appetite across different risk classes.
- A risk mandate assigns risk accountability to those at the highest levels of the firm and recognizes that business managers are the front line of risk management.
- Proper governance addresses the creation of a risk function — and associated risk committees, limits and policies — that can help control overall exposures.
- The overall risk process must be absolutely independent of the businesses generating risk; this is typically accomplished by forming an independent risk management function and developing strong internal audit practices.
- Governance must also concern itself with proper management reporting lines (particularly for those in risk-taking roles), compensation policies, education, risk communication and knowledge dissemination.
- A flawed control process is a considerable source of risk — care must be taken to ensure that no problems exist.
- Ultimately, the successful structure is based on discipline, communication and consistency.
- Elements of governance, like other dimensions of the risk management process, must be dynamic — able to adapt as market circumstances and firm-wide priorities change.

4 Risk Identification

Once a risk philosophy has been considered and a governance framework established or enhanced, the practical task of managing risk is set in motion. The first step in the process centers on the proper identification of risk — only through complete and accurate identification can a firm then measure, report and manage its exposures. The identification task may be simple or complex, depending on the nature of a firm's business, the scope of its product offerings and the extent of its geographic reach. Those responsible for identifying risks must generally examine all elements of a business or product line in order to determine how risk is generated. Risks may be created by deals, transactions, products, instruments or models, or they may arise through business or control processes. This means that all areas of the firm that have the potential to create risk — including business lines such as treasury, trading and business origination, as well as control functions such as legal, operations and settlements — must be analyzed in detail. Regardless of source, it is important for the identification phase to be as thorough as possible, as it generates the risk "roadmap" used in subsequent stages of the management process.

4.1 PROPER IDENTIFICATION OF RISK CAN ONLY OCCUR AFTER A THOROUGH UNDERSTANDING OF A PRODUCT, TRANSACTION, MARKET OR PROCESS HAS BEEN GAINED

In order to identify all dimensions of risk the target product, transaction, market or process must be thoroughly understood. Only by truly understanding how the underlying reference operates can a control officer discern different elements of risk. It is not sufficient to simply assume knowledge of how a market, product or process functions; each situation must be analyzed to learn how the reference operates and generates payoffs/liabilities. By understanding these mechanics, the control officer can isolate and identify different areas of risk. For instance, if a credit officer is asked to identify the risk of a zero-coupon payer swap (where the firm pays an annual floating rate and receives a lump sum at maturity), she must not assume that the structure functions as a standard swap, with the normal risks that characterize such an instrument; in fact, she must understand the nature of the cash flows that underpin the zero-coupon swap. After reviewing them in detail she will determine that the swap acts as an unsecured loan, generating more credit exposure than an equivalent "vanilla" structure; failure to understand the workings of the swap could result in a misidentification of risk and lead to an erroneous credit decision. Accordingly, a thorough understanding of a deal, process or reference must precede any attempt at risk identification.

4.2 ALL DIMENSIONS OF RISK MUST BE IDENTIFIED; RISKS THAT MIGHT BE LESS APPARENT AT THE TIME OF ANALYSIS SHOULD NOT BE IGNORED, AS THEY CAN BECOME MORE PROMINENT AS MARKET CONDITIONS CHANGE

Identifying risk can be very complex, particularly when it involves esoteric instruments, structures or business lines. These may carry less obvious, or "hidden," exposures that can be overlooked, and which may not become apparent until it is too late (i.e. after a loss has been sustained). Therefore, care and diligence in the identification stage is an essential requirement. In order to implement a robust identification process, qualified staff should be assigned the task of understanding, reviewing and vetting products, deals and businesses in order to discern the different types of risk that might be present—or that might arise in the future. In some cases a product or business might be relatively easy to understand and analyze; this permits risks to be identified with ease. For example, purchasing an equity option from a bank exposes a firm to a basic credit risk (the risk that the bank must perform on its obligation if the option is exercised with value) and basic market risks (the risk that changes in the underlying stock price, volatility or risk-free rate will change the value of the option). While quantifying these risks might be more challenging, the actual identification is straightforward. In other situations the risks of a product or business might be very complex, making identification much more difficult. When such complexity exists, it is advisable to consult with other experts, such as quantitative research staff or product developers. For instance, a firm might wish to deal in an exotic derivative with special payout features based on multiple asset classes. In this instance the risk function may be able to identify the presence of credit risk with relative ease, but may have more difficulty identifying all aspects of market risk; the product might be sensitive to small or large moves in each of the underlying assets, the correlations between the assets, the volatilities and cross-volatilities, and so on. Some risks might not even exist at the inception of a transaction, but may appear once particular events come to pass; the process must therefore take account of exposures that appear with the passage of time, movement of a market or triggering of some external event. For instance, if a firm purchases a knock-in option from another counterparty that has value only once a barrier is breached it must recognize that, although no risk exposure exists on trade date, exposure could arise in the future.

Properly identifying all dimensions of risk is so central to the initial stages of risk management that this concept becomes one of the "cardinal rules."

4.3 THE IDENTIFICATION PROCESS SHOULD SERVE AS THE BASE FOR THE QUANTIFICATION PROCESS; RISKS THAT ARE IDENTIFIED SHOULD BE QUANTIFIED, AND ULTIMATELY LIMITED, IN SOME MANNER

As we have noted, identification is a prerequisite for quantifying, monitoring and managing risk. When undertaking the identification process, it is important that risks uncovered be quantified and then limited. Since it is of little use to identify a series of risks and then fail to control them, the list of risks identified should form the basis for the quantification effort to follow. For example, risk officers who identify certain credit, market and liquidity risks can record them in order to quantify and limit them in subsequent stages of the process. If a firm decides not to limit a particular risk it has identified, its reasons should be properly documented in order to create an audit trail. For instance, if after analyzing a particular financial instrument a risk officer identifies five primary market risks and a negligible secondary risk (that generates almost no losses, even under virtually "unthinkable" stress tests), he may opt to limit the primary risks and not burden the process by limiting the remaining, highly insignificant, secondary risk; this should only occur once there is complete confidence that the secondary risk cannot generate any meaningful loss. If there is any lingering doubt, the exposure should obviously be capped.

4.4 THE IDENTIFICATION PROCESS SHOULD FOLLOW A LOGICAL PROGRESSION — BEGINNING WITH THE MOST COMMON OR ESSENTIAL, AND MOVING ON TO THE MORE COMPLEX OR ESOTERIC

In order not to overlook any dimensions of risk, it is helpful to first identify obvious and fundamental risks and then move to esoteric and complex risks; by following an orderly progression, a risk officer stands a better chance of identifying all relevant exposures. At the conclusion of the identification exercise the list of credit, market, liquidity, legal and operational risks should be comprehensive, and form the basis of the quantification and limit-setting phases. Expanding on the summary table in Chapter 1, we illustrate below a list of fundamental and esoteric risks a firm might encounter; the list is not, of course, comprehensive — a great deal depends on the characteristics of individual products and how a firm defines risks — but it provides a sense of the broad identification categories that must be considered.

- Credit risks
  - Fundamental
    - unsecured loan/loan-equivalent default risk
    - derivative-equivalent default risk (applicable to swaps, options, forwards, financings)
    - marketable securities/inventory default risk
    - deposit default risk
    - settlement/delivery risk
    - sovereign default risk
    - convertibility risk
    - collateral default risk
    - liquidity risk (collateral, credit)
  - Esoteric
    - cash flow mismatch risk (e.g. creating unsecured loans)
    - contingent cash flow risk (e.g. triggered by events)
    - credit cliff risk (e.g. triggered by rating events)
    - model risk (e.g. in credit analytics, pricing, valuation)
- Market risks
  - Fundamental
    - directional risk (small/large market moves, e.g. delta/gamma)
    - curve risk
    - volatility risk
    - time decay/theta risk
    - basis risk

  - correlation risk
  - spread risk
  - devaluation risk
  - concentration risk
  - liquidity risk (asset, funding)
- Esoteric
  - skew risk
  - cross-gamma risk
  - cross-volatility risk
  - volatility of volatility risk
  - model risk (e.g. in market analytics, pricing, valuation)

4.5 IN THE SEARCH FOR MORE COMPLEX DIMENSIONS OF RISK, CARE MUST BE TAKEN NOT TO OVERLOOK THE MOST OBVIOUS RISKS

A corollary to the rule above suggests that when scrutinizing complex dimensions of risk, care must be taken not to ignore obvious exposures. While thorough analysis of a product or deal should ultimately reveal complex credit or market risks, fundamental risks might also exist. Consider a case where a firm is entering a new market to trade local government authority bonds. The risk officer in charge of the analysis might determine that the local bonds are exposed to the changing direction and shape of the yield curve. In addition, since the bonds are callable, they might feature a degree of option risk, and since they trade at a spread to the country's government bonds, they might feature spread risk against government hedges. Having identified these important core risks, the risk officer might then engage in stress testing to quantify some maximum likely downside scenario, and then establish limits that constrain exposures that have been identified. While this is sensible, and indicative of the type of effort that is required to identify, and subsequently limit, risks, the officer may have forgotten one very obvious exposure: rather than settling within five days, as is customary in the risk officer's own home bond market, the local bonds may settle on a 30-day basis. This fundamental, but vital, dimension of risk can generate incremental credit exposure, as any seller/buyer of bonds the firm deals with will have up to 30 days of market moves before settling on a deal — sufficient time to generate considerable credit exposure and, in the event of default, credit loss. Thus, while the search for less obvious risks may turn up important factors, more fundamental exposures must not be overlooked.

4.6 RISK IDENTIFICATION SHOULD BE AN ONGOING PROCESS THAT CONTINUALLY RE-EXAMINES ALL DIMENSIONS OF EXPOSURE

Since financial markets are dynamic, it is important that individual stages in the risk management process be flexible — risks may change with time or market circumstances. Accordingly, a risk identification process should allow for continuous re-examination of exposures. By creating a process that allows risk managers and business leaders to revisit risks, a firm ensures that it is not neglecting, understating or overstating its exposures as the environment changes.

For instance, if a firm enters into a commodity derivative market that permits physical (but not financial) delivery of an underlying commodity, it identifies, and subsequently manages, dimensions of risk associated with physical settlement of the commodity. If, one year later, the market characteristics change and the commodity derivative allows for financial, as well as physical, delivery, the firm may be able to lower its risk exposures by shifting its dealings to net financial settlement; by re-examining the changing characteristics of the marketplace, the firm has been able to "re-identify," and thereby reduce, its risk exposures. A firm may choose to formalize a process of continuous identification by setting annual review targets for each business. Alternatively, it may rely on an ad-hoc method, leaving the matter with individual business managers and risk officers. Any mechanism that operates effectively is likely to be adequate. It is worth stressing that the review discipline must apply to business control processes as well as actual business products/lines.

4.7 RISK OFFICERS SHOULD WORK WITH TRADERS, PRODUCT EXPERTS AND FINANCE PERSONNEL TO ANALYZE PRODUCTS AND IDENTIFY RISKS

An extension to the rule above indicates that, when necessary, risk officers should engage others to help in the identification process. In fact, seeking assistance from "experts" should be encouraged, as it can increase the accuracy of the process. Those with different perspectives or skills may help identify pockets of risk that might not be apparent to the risk or control officer. Quantitative research staff and trading/business managers responsible for creating new products can be especially helpful in this regard. As they construct a product, and model it in order to understand risk dynamics and pricing sensitivities, they are likely to come in contact with all of its risk parameters. Risk officers can thus take advantage of work that has been done by business personnel. The obvious caveat is that even business "experts" might not always be able to identify all dimensions of risk. For instance, trading managers, accustomed to dealing with market and liquidity risks, might find credit, legal or operational risk exposures outside their domain of expertise. Likewise, investment bankers dealing with capital commitments, financings and underwritings may be very comfortable dealing with credit risks, but might find market and liquidity risks somewhat alien. It is worth noting that in addition to business unit leaders and quantitative specialists, those in control functions, including audit, finance, legal and operations, can share a useful perspective on risk identification.

As indicated in Chapters 2 and 3, the risk governance structure often allows for the creation of a new product review process. This can be a good forum for the initial review and identification of exposures, and can be used to consider scenarios where new, or latent, risks might appear. Once identified, it is good practice to document the findings; this helps ensure that all risks are properly limited during a subsequent phase in the process. It also serves as an important component of the internal/external audit trail, and can be useful when discussing the risk process with regulatory authorities.

4.8 RISK SPECIALISTS MUST FOCUS ON DETAILS BECAUSE THE DISCIPLINE IS COMPLEX; BUT REVIEWING BROADER "MACRO" ISSUES IS ALSO AN IMPORTANT PART OF THE RISK PROCESS

Risk specialists are vital in a world of complex risks; a focus on, and attention to, detail is important. This helps ensure that less obvious risks are identified and managed, and that a thorough understanding of the portfolio is undertaken. However, focusing solely on detail can cause a specialist to miss broader risk dynamics that might be at work. This can have unfortunate consequences, as ignoring the broad operating environment and overall mosaic of risks can lead to a misidentification of risk and erroneous actions. For instance, if a credit officer covering the utility sector becomes an expert on the creditworthiness of 15 utility companies, but fails to examine how interest rates, deregulation, new power supply and other macro events are impacting the overall creditworthiness and credit exposure of the companies, he may lose out on very valuable information — information that could alter the decision-making process on future deals. Devoting time and resources to analyzing and understanding the macro environment is thus important.

4.9 COOPERATION BETWEEN DIFFERENT CONTROL UNITS CAN LEAD TO IDENTIFICATION OF RISKS THAT "CROSS BOUNDARIES"

Although most business risks can be defined and categorized quite explicitly (e.g. credit risk, market risk, and so forth) there are instances where risk can cross disciplines and control structures. In such cases it is good practice for those impacted to be cognizant of the "cross boundary" nature of the risk and make sure exposure is properly identified and managed. Failure to do so may lead to uneven treatment; some units may manage the risk in one fashion, while others may take a completely different approach — the inconsistency may, itself, create a greater risk of loss. One area where "cross boundary" exposure can appear is in operational, or process, risk. It is quite common for individual businesses to feature their own settlement, clearing and financial control functions (e.g. a derivative desk might feature its own support units, a bond desk its own units, and so forth). To ensure consistency in the treatment of common operational risks (e.g. settlement errors, past-due confirmations, data failures, and so on) control officers from each dedicated unit should work together to identify and then manage these common risks.

4.10 ALL SOURCES OF SETTLEMENT RISK MUST BE IDENTIFIED

Participants in the financial system are becoming increasingly attuned to the concept of settlement, or delivery, risk and should seek to identify it in different products and markets. Settlement risk arises from timing differences related to the receipt and disbursement of cash and/or securities. Though settlement risk is commonly associated with the foreign exchange market, where the release of currency in one market/time zone may not coincide with the receipt of currency in another time zone (creating an intraday or overnight risk exposure), it is also evident in other markets; dealing in certain local government bond and equity markets, for instance, can create settlement risk lasting several hours or days. It is especially important to consider the presence of settlement risk in new or unfamiliar local markets, which may have unique cash/securities settlement characteristics that do not adhere to basic "delivery against cash/receipt against payment" rules. Since firms have suffered losses as a result of such risk (e.g. in the cases of Herstatt Bank in Germany, BCCI in Luxembourg, and others), risk officers must ensure that instruments or deals they are considering are reviewed for settlement risk. In the extreme, failure to properly identify positions that carry such risk can result in open exposures of some magnitude; during times of crisis or default, these exposures may generate losses. While the advent of computerized trading platforms and electronic clearing and settlement systems has improved considerably over the past few years new efforts at creating more automated clearing/settlement of foreign exchange and bonds, for instance, have not yet yielded a secure framework. Accordingly, a thorough understanding of the settlement rules that can give rise to risk is an essential component of the identification process.

4.11 HEDGES MAY NOT ALWAYS FUNCTION AS INTENDED; POTENTIAL "PROBLEM HEDGES" SHOULD BE IDENTIFIED IN ADVANCE

A firm typically creates a hedge in order to mitigate, minimize or neutralize the amount of risk on its books; a well-constructed hedge, of reasonable size, can be effective in achieving this risk management goal. However, there may be instances where a hedge is not properly constructed and fails to provide the benefits sought. A hedge may fail to work for various reasons: the match between the hedge and reference instrument may be imperfect (giving rise to basis risk), the historical relationship (or correlation) between the two instruments may break down or decouple, the hedge may be too large for the market to absorb, the legal terms covering the two instruments may not match, and so on. For instance, a firm that has traditionally used Treasury bonds to hedge its mortgage backed securities portfolio may have experienced poor hedge performance during particular markets and interest rate cycles; identifying and tracking this potential hedge problem might lead it to create an alternate strategy based on swaps rather than Treasuries. Alternatively, if a firm is hedging a very large position in a commodity through the listed futures market, it may be required to "stack and roll" the hedge in the short-end of the curve, where liquidity is greatest. If the position is so large that the firm cannot rehedge as contracts mature, it creates a growing risk exposure; in addition, any adverse movement in the long-end of the curve might generate incremental losses. Risk officers should work closely with trading and business managers during the identification stage to highlight large, imperfect or complex hedges that might expose the firm to additional risk in the event of a breakdown. Once identified, the downside of a problem hedge can be quantified and managed through conservative risk allocation or establishment of reserves. The efficacy of any "difficult" hedges that have been identified should, of course, be tested and reviewed on a regular basis.

4.12 RISK ARISING FROM CONVERGENCE/DIVERGENCE TRADES MUST BE IDENTIFIED

Certain institutions take positions in assets that are expected to converge (or diverge) over a period of time. These trading strategies are often considered "lower risk" as they typically involve taking a long position in one asset and a short position in another—to the extent convergence or divergence occurs as anticipated, much of the directional risk of the strategy may be removed. In fact, such transactions may be very high risk (and particularly damaging if leveraged). Convergence/divergence strategies are generally based on the magnitude/direction of correlations between reference assets; these correlations can become unstable in the face of a crisis, causing seemingly low-risk trades to generate large exposures. For instance, if a firm executes a bond convergence trade, expecting the spread between two bonds to tighten until they are equal, but market circumstances cause the spread to widen instead (perhaps as a result of liquidity problems, credit pressures, or some other factor), it actually has risk on both positions. If the strategy is leveraged or illiquid, the firm may have difficulty unwinding without suffering a considerable loss. Since these types of trades are often considered low risk, they might be overlooked in favor of transactions with more obvious risks. Accordingly, the identification process should focus on proposed convergence or divergence products or business lines to ensure that the strategies and correlation effects are well understood. Strategies that are identified should be actively monitored and managed in subsequent phases of the risk process.

4.13 MODELS USED TO PRICE AND MANAGE RISKS MAY CONTAIN RISKS OF THEIR OWN

Companies active in any type of financial engineering — including product development, market-making or hedging/risk management of exposures — are likely to employ financial instruments that are valued using models. Such models, as noted in Chapter 1, are based on financial mathematics of varying degrees of complexity; most also require the use of simplifying assumptions that reduce computing time or deal with known market limitations. As we shall discuss in Chapter 5, employing complex mathematics and assumptions to create models introduces the concept of "model risk" — the risk that a firm will suffer losses as a result of mathematical misspecifications or misapplication of assumptions. Such model risk is quite real. For instance, in 1997 Bank of Tokyo Mitsubishi indicated that it had lost $83MM as a result of model error; in the same year National Westminster Bank (now part of Royal Bank of Scotland) posted $139MM in model-related losses. Since model risk can be as damaging as any other class of risk, it must be identified and controlled. Once limitations or errors have been identified they can be amended or protected through reserves or conservative risk treatment. For instance, if a firm actively deals in interest rate derivatives, it may use various interest rate risk models to generate curves and valuations. In reviewing the underlying analytics, the risk professional responsible for model analysis may discover a flaw in the valuation of interest rate options in a low (or zero) interest rate environment; having identified this as a potential risk, he may propose a correction to the underlying mathematics used to value interest rate options. The identification of model risk is not simple. Since models are based on quantitative processes, understanding potential flaws requires a high degree of numeracy. Accordingly, those charged with identifying shortcomings generated by risk models must be skilled in financial mathematics.

4.14 RISK EXPOSURES CREATED THROUGH CHANGES IN THE STRUCTURE AND TIMING OF CASH FLOWS MUST BE IDENTIFIED

Examination of cash flow patterns associated with a product, structure or deal is an integral part of the risk identification process. The nature and timing of cash flows can have a considerable impact on the risk profile of a deal; this is particularly true for credit risk exposures, where the simple alteration of cash flow timing can create unsecured credit risk. For instance, if a firm is entering into an unsecured, delayed-start swap that requires it to pay a certain sum at inception of the deal but receive no net payment until the first anniversary, it has effectively extended a one-year unsecured loan to its counterparty. An even more extreme example occurs in the case of an unsecured, multi-year, zero-coupon swap, where one firm makes periodic semi-annual or annual payments, but the second firm makes no payments until the conclusion of the transaction — effectively borrowing on an unsecured basis for the tenor of the swap. Though the terminology and structure suggest these might be standard derivative transactions, a risk officer who reviews the timing of the cash flows will identify the existence of incremental risk exposure. Contingent cash flows — those which are payable or receivable once a given event has occurred — are another popular form of altering the timing of payments; these can also change the shape of the firm's risk profile and must be scrutinized. Correctly identifying cash flows allows "synthetic" loan exposures to be controlled and monitored and appropriate credit risk premiums to be charged.

4.15 NEW PRODUCTS AND MARKETS CAN CONTAIN SPECIAL RISKS THAT HAVE NOT BEEN ENCOUNTERED BEFORE; THESE RISKS SHOULD BE THOROUGHLY UNDERSTOOD

As noted, a new product review process allows control officers to examine the risk characteristics of new markets, businesses and products. A new product (or business) is generally defined to be new to a firm, and may also be new to the marketplace. The firm might be assuming risks that is has never before dealt with and may, in fact, need new ways of identifying, measuring, monitoring and managing these risks. For example, if a company decides that it wants to create, for the first time, a dedicated financial treasury unit to manage interest rate and currency risks associated with its core business operations, it may conduct a new product review so that business and control officials can discuss the markets/products, system requirements, processing/settling mechanisms, end-of-day position, P&L and risk reporting routines, credit, market and legal risk requirements, capital allocation methods, and so forth. The forum should serve to highlight where the true risks reside and how they will be controlled. Vetting must always be comprehensive so that all risks can be properly identified. Approvals should not be granted until risk officers (and others operating in control functions) are satisfied that the review has been thorough and that all potential risks have been identified and addressed. While attention to detail is critical, this should not be an excuse for creating a bureaucratic, time-consuming process that delays the introduction of a product or initiative. New products should be reviewed and discussed as quickly and efficiently as possible; when additional requirements or controls are deemed necessary, these should be communicated immediately.

4.16 LOCAL MARKETS MAY POSSESS VERY UNIQUE RISKS AND DUE CARE MUST BE TAKEN TO UNDERSTAND THEM

An institution takes comfort in dealing in its "home market." Conventions, terms and practices may be well understood and, while they may present risk challenges, are unlikely to create "surprises." The same may not necessarily be true in local markets that are foreign to a firm; in such cases, thorough analysis of conventions and practices is advisable. Only through a very thorough and methodical analysis is a risk officer likely to isolate and identify what may be unique risk exposures. If, as noted above, entry into a local market is part of a firm's new product process, the same type of analytical/due diligence template can be applied in the identification of risk exposures. For instance, if a firm is considering trading local corporate and government bonds in an emerging market, the market and credit risk officers must identify all relevant risks. The market risk officer might identify risk exposures generated by lack of liquidity, the direction and volatility of interest rates, the shape of the yield curve, the spread against government bonds and the basis against local bond futures. The credit officer might identify sovereign or corporate default risk, as well as convertibility risk; in addition, knowing that the settlement period for bonds is 15 days, the credit officer might identify forward credit risk exposure on the sale or purchase of bonds. Other control functions might identify unique sources of risk, including legal capital risk (risk that the firm might be required to pledge capital to the local market for a set number of years before it can be withdrawn), physical settlement risk (risk that securities trading settles in physical, rather than electronic, form, leading to the possibility of fraud or error), and so on. Since every local market features very unique characteristics, a process to thoroughly identify exposures is essential.

4.17 "RISK-FREE" STRATEGIES WITH ABOVE AVERAGE RETURNS ARE RARELY RISK-FREE; POCKETS OF "HIDDEN" OR STRUCTURAL RISK MAY EXIST

It is not uncommon for traders, originators, bankers or business leaders to speak of a "risk-free" strategy, deal or business; care should be taken when evaluating such proposals. While risk-free strategies may exist, they are unlikely to generate risk-free profits in excess of what can be earned in true risk-free markets (e.g. the US Treasury bond market). In a world of easily accessible information and arbitrage forces, any risk-free strategy characterized by above average returns will be exploited very rapidly. This suggests two alternate scenarios: the risk-free strategy is not really risk-free, meaning that pockets of "hidden" or unrecognized risk may exist (a fact which astute risk managers should be able to discern given sufficient information and analytic capabilities); or the returns promised are not really above average, but precisely equal to those that can be obtained in other risk-free markets. Accordingly, a thorough investigation of risk-free strategies is advisable. For instance, a trader might believe that if he intermediates between two different participants — taking a flow from one and passing it to the other, and vice versa, for a fee — he is earning a risk-free return. Under this scenario, however, the firm is almost certain to be acting as a principal, rather than agent or broker; thus, if one party fails to perform, the firm must still perform on its portion of the transaction — indicating that the strategy is not risk-free, but one with elements of credit risk. A careful understanding of "risk-free" strategies must therefore be undertaken before committing capital.

4.18 IF THE IDENTIFICATION PROCESS REVEALS THAT A LARGE NUMBER OF FIRMS ARE EXTENDING CREDIT TO A COUNTERPARTY, CAUTION SHOULD BE EXERCISED

Past financial crises have demonstrated that when a single counterparty is doing business with a great number of financial firms — and the industry as a whole is aware of it — complications may arise. A single counterparty that has arranged credit terms with a large number of firms in order to replicate trading or investment positions with each of them commands considerable systemic leverage. Such leverage may create credit difficulties if markets or strategies move against the counterparty; this, as demonstrated by the Orange County and LTCM crises, can have broader system-wide implications and may ultimately result in substantial losses for those involved. Accordingly, during the risk identification process it is important for the credit officer to probe the nature of the counterparty's credit relationships, how it utilizes leverage and what strategies it favors. If a concentration is identified, exposures should be minimized or secured; even when secured, prudent standards must be applied.

4.19 THE EXISTENCE OF "CREDIT CLIFFS" CAN RESULT IN THE CREATION OF SUB-INVESTMENT GRADE CREDIT EXPOSURES, AND SHOULD BE IDENTIFIED IN ADVANCE

A "credit cliff" exists whenever a credit issuer or counterparty faces the prospect of a large, and sudden, change in credit quality. When a credit cliff is traversed, investment grade exposures become sub-investment grade, placing creditor firms in a more precarious financial position. Credit cliffs must be identified in advance so that they can be monitored and limited; failure to do so can lead to the assumption of unsecured, sub-investment grade credit exposure or, in the extreme, outright losses due to counterparty default. Credit cliffs can be generated by a number of factors. For instance, a counterparty might receive a higher rating based on the presence of financial support from a parent, insurer or third-party guarantor; absent the financial support, the counterparty might not be sufficiently creditworthy to warrant the higher rating. Accordingly, any withdrawal of the support will cause an immediate downgrade of the counterparty—perhaps to sub-investment grade levels. Alternatively, a counterparty might be considered an investment grade credit based on its access to liquidity and funding; this is especially true for financial and trading businesses which rely on liquidity, funding and the confidence of trading partners in order to conduct business. If any of these factors becomes impaired, the credit perception of the counterparty can fall very rapidly. This generates a self-fulfilling spiral: lack of confidence causes liquidity to be withdrawn, leading to a further loss of confidence and the withdrawal of more liquidity, and so forth, until default. A credit cliff might also arise if a counterparty has certain external rating triggers which require it to take particular financial actions in the event of a downgrade; in taking such actions, the counterparty's financial position may deteriorate further, causing more downgrades and a spiral into default. For instance, if a counterparty is required to post collateral or liquidate assets and repay debt in the event of a downgrade, it may find itself in a weaker financial state at the conclusion—this may precipitate a further round of downgrades and could culminate in default. Regardless of the specific mechanism that might cause a credit cliff to be breached, each one should be identified in advance.

4.20 MARKET RISK CONCENTRATIONS MUST BE PROPERLY IDENTIFIED

Concentrated risk positions can result in significant market losses if not managed properly; in order to manage concentrations it is first necessary to identify them. In most cases it is relatively easy to locate concentrations. This is particularly true when a firm structures its risk-taking in an organized and disciplined fashion, so that identical risks are managed by a single center; under this structure no other trading or business units can assume the same risks, making identification simple. Thus, if a firm channels all US corporate bond trading through a single desk in New York, it can easily identify all US corporate bond risk concentrations. Complexity increases when firms permit different desks to trade across multiple risk classes, or when a firm deals in products that generate residual risks. For instance, if a firm's corporate bond trading desks in New York, London, Tokyo and Singapore are permitted to deal in US corporate bonds, the identification of a concentrated position now involves the aggregation of positions across locations (and perhaps different trading technology platforms); this is more time-consuming and, if technology is not robust, prone to error. A firm trading products that create residual, or second order, risks may also have greater difficulty identifying concentrations without undertaking a complicated aggregation process. For example, if a bank is active in equity, interest rate and currency derivatives, its primary interest rate exposures will be generated by the interest rate derivatives desk, while residual interest rate exposures will exist on the other two desks (e.g. interest rate exposure is a by-product of dealing in instruments with optionality and those based on forward curves); in order to determine a concentrated US or Euro interest rate risk position, the firm needs to identify the fact that all three desks carry the risk and must then aggregate the positions across multiple technology platforms — this may be a difficult task.

4.21 UNDERSTANDING AND IDENTIFYING THE LINKS BETWEEN LIQUIDITY, LEVERAGE, FUNDING AND EXPOSURE IS VITAL

Financial crises often reveal linkages between leverage, liquidity and exposure. Leverage, which may be on- or off-balance sheet, magnifies gains and losses. If a firm has a $100MM bond position and the position falls by 5%, it loses $5MM; if it uses the $100MM bond and pledges it as security under a financing arrangement to buy a further $100MM of bonds, it has accumulated a $200MM position for the same original $100MM investment. A 5% drop now translates into a $10MM loss. Multiples of leverage, on the order of 25 or 50 times, are not uncommon among financial institutions, hedge funds and other highly leveraged institutions — particularly during market booms, when memories of financial crises have waned. The more leveraged an institution, the more sensitive it is to market prices. Liquidity, which influences prices, can cause a highly leveraged firm to lose money quickly. If a market dislocation causes sudden illiquidity in a particular asset, the price may gap down rapidly and cause a loss; the effects of leverage magnify the price gap, creating a larger amount of exposure to the firm extending credit, and potentially large losses to the firm using the leverage. Understanding how these dynamics operate, and identifying situations where they may exist, is central to the prudent extension of credit. The same linkages can also appear in funding. If a highly leveraged firm with an illiquid book is forced to repay maturing financing, it may create a spiral as it sells increasingly illiquid assets in a downward falling market — selling into illiquidity simply drives the price down further, resulting in insufficient funds to repay loans, necessitating the liquidation of more collateral, and so on. Once again, a mechanism to ensure identification and review of liquidity and exposure is vital. As noted later in the book, any prudent measure of risk exposure must accurately depict losses that might arise from a stressed situation — one characterized by market volatility, illiquidity and leverage. Risk officers, knowing that leverage, liquidity, funding and exposure are often related, must identify instances where these relationships exist; correct identification allows proper control measures to be instituted.

4.22 DURING TIMES OF MARKET STRESS, MARKET AND CREDIT RISKS CAN BECOME LINKED; ADVANCE IDENTIFICATION OF THESE LINKAGES CAN HELP AVOID PROBLEMS

Market and credit risks often merge during times of market stress, compounding potential losses; identifying how, where and when these linkages might occur can help a firm avoid, or minimize, potential losses. Credit and market risks can become linked in at least three different ways. First, as markets move sharply, the market value of a credit exposure can change dramatically. If that exposure is linked to an actual counterparty (e.g. in the form of a credit extension, such as a derivative or financing), the counterparty's ability to perform might be impaired — this is primarily true for very highly leveraged or uncreditworthy counterparties. Second, when market stress occurs, liquidity often disappears; the absence of liquidity can lead to a deterioration in the market value of the underlying assets, compounding the size of counterparty credit exposure. Third, during market stress any collateral taken to secure a counterparty exposure may be impacted — particularly when the security is in the form of corporate securities or other instruments with high price volatility. In such instances the market value of the collateral might deteriorate to the point where it is insufficient to cover credit exposure, leaving a firm with a previously secured exposure partially, or totally, unsecured. These linkages were demonstrated during the 1998 hedge fund crisis, when funds (including LTCM) built up very large, leveraged positions in a number of markets. As markets deteriorated, the credit exposure extended by banks to funds increased — precisely as their creditworthiness deteriorated. Furthermore, collateral taken by banks to secure trades was liquidated as exposures grew and credit quality declined; however, collateral was sold into a thin market, leaving some banks with insufficient proceeds to cover their exposure. Identifying market and credit risk linkages, and how the links might perform during times of market stress, is an important part of the risk identification process.

4.23 RISK OUTSIDE A SPECIALIST'S DOMAIN THAT IS DISCOVERED DURING THE IDENTIFICATION STAGE SHOULD BE FORWARDED TO A UNIT WITH DIRECT RESPONSIBILITY

Exposure outside a risk specialist's domain that is encountered during the identification phase should be forwarded to those who may have more direct responsibility; this helps ensure that all risks are properly considered. Business managers often consult with risk officers in order to obtain preliminary feedback and guidance on new products/structures. As a result, a risk officer may encounter unique aspects of risk that fall outside the traditional market or credit risk domain; in such cases, issues should be forwarded to the relevant control officer. In the absence of a formal new product review process, a risk officer should not assume that risk issues will be forwarded by business leaders to the appropriate control officers — it is wiser for the risk officer to alert colleagues. For instance, a risk manager reviewing the market risk dimensions of a new structured bond/derivative package that utilizes a special purpose vehicle may note that the structure contains very specific legal issues associated with the creation of the vehicle and the perfection of a security interest in collateral underlying the vehicle. Knowing that these legal issues are potentially significant, the risk manager forwards the transaction details to her colleague in the legal department, who can use his expertise to evaluate the legal risk ramifications of the structure. Being proactive in elevating risk issues to those who are best able to manage them strengthens the overall risk control process.

4.24 IDENTIFYING THE SOURCE OF THE NEXT "LARGE LOSS" CAN PROVIDE GUIDANCE ON THE NATURE/QUALITY OF CONTROLS NEEDED TO PROTECT AGAINST SUCH A LOSS

While the credit, market, legal and operational risk management disciplines are reasonably well-defined and focused on set issues, concerns and variables, a firm should always prepare for the "unexpected" by considering how else it might suffer a large loss; this type of creative thinking forces it to constantly question different aspects of the business and control infrastructure. It is well known that an institution active in bond trading can lose money from changes in the direction of interest rates and volatility, the shape of the yield curve, or the movement of credit spreads or the basis; a market risk manager is expected to know this and set appropriate limits to capture potential downside exposure. The same must occur with credit risks. However, a firm must also consider other areas where it might lose money. Perhaps it is exposed to significant client suitability, documentation or capital commitment risks. Perhaps the departure of one or two key members of a trading team, with particularly detailed knowledge of complex risks residing within a book, can create an exposure. Or maybe the firm's infrastructure is too inflexible to accommodate the "next generation" of risk products. Regardless of the nature of the risk or the area that it impacts, this type of "blue-sky thinking" can create an important control awareness within the organization. Linking results from this type of identification exercise with actual control requirements can help a firm prepare for a potential disaster scenario.

4.25 IF AN UNEXPECTED LOSS OCCURS, THE IDENTIFICATION PROCESS MAY NOT BE WORKING CORRECTLY AND SHOULD BE REVIEWED

The identification stage of the risk process exists in order to highlight every potential source of risk facing a firm; this permits it to quantify, limit and manage exposures. If a firm sustains a loss that is larger than expected, it may need to review its quantification or management techniques to determine whether too much risk capacity has been granted or if the underlying risk analytics/models contain errors; such an event would be indicative of potential weaknesses in governance or quantification, rather than identification. However, if a firm sustains a loss from an unexpected source, the identification process may be flawed and must be redesigned so that it is truly effective. For example, if a bank starts trading in cross-commodity options and has identified a range of risks — delta, gamma, theta, volatility, interest rate, and so on — which it then limits, it should not be surprised if it sustains a loss in any of these risk categories. However, if the bank loses money when it readjusts the correlation matrix used to value the options because it failed to identify, and then quantify and limit, its exposure to correlation risk, then its identification process is inadequate; it must be redesigned so that it captures all risks. The redesign may require greater participation by those with "expert" knowledge of particular businesses or scrutiny by the audit function. Misidentification of risk can remain a weak link in the risk management process and must be corrected.

Summarizing the simple rules of the identification process, we note the following:

- It is important to thoroughly understand the functioning of a product, business or process in order to be able to identify different dimensions of risk.
- The identification process must be continuous, as risk can change as markets, products and counterparties evolve.
- Where necessary, those responsible for identifying risks should seek help from quantitative or product specialists, who may already be familiar with different aspects of exposure.
- Identification must involve a search for obvious and complex risks, as well as those that change over time.

- In addition to relatively standard market and credit risks, the identification process should focus on risks that might exist in other areas; these might include settlement risk, hedge risk, convergence/divergence risk, concentration risk, local market risk, model risk, cash flow structure risk, and so on.
- It is helpful to speculate on other positions or processes that might generate large losses in the future; if any "new pockets" of risk are identified, they should be reviewed from a control perspective.
- When risks that reside outside of a specialist's area of expertise are identified, they should be forwarded to those with more direct responsibility.
- If a loss from an unexpected source occurs, the identification process should be reviewed, as it may indicate a flaw.

5
Risk Quantification and Analysis

We have noted at various points that the effective risk management process relies on tools and skills from the quantitative and qualitative sectors; the quantification stage of the risk management process brings the two together to create the strongest possible risk framework. In order to manage exposures that have been identified, risk and trading managers need to understand the magnitude of the risks they are facing; this can be done by using financial mathematics to create analytics that allow for proper quantification. In some cases the quantification effort is simple and precise. For instance, in order to determine the interest rate risk of a Treasury bond, traders and risk officers can make use of duration and convexity formulas, which produce very exact results. In other cases the exercise is more difficult, and may be subjective. When dealing with diversified portfolios of risk, long-dated structures or complex cross-asset derivatives, for instance, there may be no precise way of quantifying risk exposures. While analytics can be created to generate price and risk estimates for such exposures, they are ultimately based on financial mathematics that depend on a variety of assumptions. Errors in the financial mathematics, or underlying assumptions, give rise to "model risk," and the potential for model-related losses.

Firms employing portfolio or derivative valuation tools must understand the nature of the assumptions and limitations that impact quantitative processes, and factor them into the decision-making framework. For instance, VAR, which has emerged as a de-facto "industry standard" for estimating the amount of market risk inherent in a portfolio, is based on numerous assumptions that can render the measure "error prone." In implementing a VAR methodology a firm makes certain assumptions related to the methodology — including the distribution of returns, magnitude/direction of correlations, and so forth — which may, or may not, be credible. If a firm assumes that financial returns are distributed normally when they are actually characterized by skewness and "fat tails," disaster events will happen more often than predicted and may be much larger than expected. In addition, if a firm assumes that the correlations between risks in the portfolio are of a particular size, any substantive change during a market dislocation will generate results that are different than those anticipated. Such concerns are not limited to VAR models; the same is also true for other quantitative measures. Thus, while the quantitative discipline is of vital importance in risk management, it must be approached with full knowledge of limitations. By recognizing the potential shortcomings, a firm can calibrate its processes and generate useful risk measures.

5.1 RISKS DISCOVERED IN THE IDENTIFICATION STAGES SHOULD BE DECOMPOSED INTO QUANTIFIABLE TERMS; THIS ALLOWS EXPOSURES TO BE CONSTRAINED AND MONITORED

Once the identification of product or business risks has occurred, the risk officer can quantify relevant risks; this ultimately permits establishment of limits and monitoring of exposures. We have indicated that during the identification stage it is important not to overlook any risks; this holds true in the quantification stage, where it is vital to decompose risks that have been identified into quantifiable terms. Even the most complex structures, products and deals can be decomposed into terms that allow for quantification. For instance, if a firm is preparing to underwrite a complicated project financing, the credit officer needs to dissect the cash flow streams and structural enhancements to determine where the credit risk resides and how large the exposure might become under particular scenarios. The risk manager considering a new complex derivative — perhaps a compound option that is "quanto'ed" (or exchanged) into a foreign currency — needs to identify various market risk dimensions in the initial stage (delta, gamma, cross-gamma, volatility, and so on) and can then quantify the effect each component has on the deal (or portfolio of deals). The quantification stage is not trivial — it is a very rigorous process that generally requires highly numerate risk officers with considerable analytic skills. However, even the most complex product or deal can typically be dissected into quantifiable components.

5.2 THOUGH CERTAIN RISKS CAN BE DIFFICULT TO QUANTIFY, BASIC ATTEMPTS AT MEASUREMENT ARE IMPORTANT IN ORDER TO OBTAIN AN INDICATION OF RISKINESS

Though many risks are relatively easy to quantify, some can be very challenging and difficult. When a very complex quantification problem arises, attempts at quantification must still be made — this provides a general level of riskiness and ultimately helps in the decision-making process. In general, techniques for quantifying credit and market risks are quite well established. Quantifying operational risk (i.e. risk related to failure of internal control processes/platforms (e.g. fraud, error, disaster, non-functioning systems, and so forth) is far less established and often more challenging. Most firms lack sufficient large loss data to properly model the behavior of such risks (e.g. lack of data does not permit the collection of a representative sample, making construction of a loss distribution difficult); accordingly, operational risks are often difficult to quantify. Despite the relative complexity, creating a basic process to estimate losses over time is an acceptable way of implementing a metric; the metric can then be enhanced and modified as data becomes more robust or new techniques are developed. For instance, a firm may wish to collect loss data from its own operating units and combine it with publicized loss data from the industry at large. It may then construct a distribution of operating risk based on high probability, low severity losses (e.g. internal losses) and enhance it by incorporating low probability, high severity losses (e.g. internal or external losses) — this gives the distribution a more realistic appearance, incorporating "fat tails" that can skew loss estimates. Thereafter it can determine how much capital to apply to the mean and extreme points on the curve. While by no means perfect, such a process represents an attempt to quantify exposure that is difficult to measure and can give a firm important insight into the magnitude of the risk it might be facing.

5.3 MODELS ARE BASED ON ASSUMPTIONS THAT MAY, OR MAY NOT, BE REALISTIC; ASSUMPTIONS, AND THE IMPACT THEY CAN HAVE ON VALUATION, MUST BE WELL UNDERSTOOD

Models are the financial cornerstone of trading and risk management — they make possible deal pricing, exposure quantification, stress testing and risk management. There is no denying the power and utility of financial models in the risk management framework. That said, models have limitations that can give rise to model risk; failure to recognize limitations may ultimately lead to financial losses. Many models are created by making simplifying assumptions. Such assumptions may be necessary in order to obtain a reasonable result, eliminate extraneous information, or create an efficient computing process. Some of these assumptions may be reasonable in the context of a single trade/product or within simple portfolios. In other cases, assumptions might be unrealistic, or even flawed, when applied to complex products or larger portfolios. When this occurs (or is believed to occur) the assumptions must be thoroughly reviewed. The assumptions should be stressed in order to understand how they impact different elements of a trade or portfolio; alternate assumptions should also be considered, to verify how outputs change. A full review of any model impacting the risk discipline — including those that generate prices, pricing variables, finance outputs, risk sensitivities, hedging ratios and other risk information — must therefore be reviewed and documented by the independent risk function. Shortcomings should be noted and, where relevant, covered by an appropriate, and agreed, model reserve; since financial modeling is not perfect, establishment of reserves emerges as a prudent measure.

As we have noted, many institutions have employed VAR models since the mid-1990s in order to quantify the market risk of single or multiple businesses. VAR models, which can be created in various ways (e.g. variance/covariance, historical simulation, Monte Carlo simulation) indicate how much money might be earned or lost based on the size of the position, the length of the holding period and the level of statistical confidence. While VAR has been adopted by institutions and regulators as a reasonable tool for identifying and aggregating risks, VAR models have limitations and weaknesses. As noted earlier, VAR relies on assumptions about the distribution of the underlying asset reference prices, the length of the holding period and magnitude of correlations; each of these might break down during times of crisis. In addition, VAR, by virtue of its construction, cannot indicate how much a firm might lose for any observation in excess of the confidence level selected; in some cases losses might be very significant (as witnessed during 1998, for example). Thus, while VAR may be an acceptable tool for the general quantification and aggregation of a portfolio of market risks, it has limitations and relies heavily on assumptions; these must be recognized and factored into the management process.

5.4 MODELS SHOULD NOT BE USED TO THE POINT OF "BLIND FAITH" — THEY ARE ONLY ANCILLARY TOOLS INTENDED TO SUPPLEMENT THE RISK PROCESS

A corollary to the rule above indicates that a firm must avoid taking false comfort in the power of models. The firm that utilizes models blindly — to consider and conduct all aspects of risk management — is unlikely to create a successful, and enduring, risk process. Since models have limitations — and, in some cases, considerable flaws — using them to drive the risk management process exposes the firm to losses every time limitations or errors are revealed. A series of model losses can erode the credibility of the risk function and reduce its effectiveness. If a firm actively involved in derivatives uses models to provide valuations, risk sensitivities, stress tests, hypothetical reserve calculations, risk-adjusted return estimates, credit exposure and VAR — and accepts all the results as given, without question — it may be placing far too much faith in the power and capacity of the underlying models to manage risk and make risk-related recommendations (or decisions). A firm that utilizes models as one of many tools in its risk management "toolbox" is far more likely to achieve success in its risk process. When a model produces risk information that is very sensitive to underlying assumptions, the risk officer must interpret the results in the context of known deficiencies or limitations. When this discipline exists, models become important tools in the risk process; when it does not exist, a firm may be exposing itself too heavily to model risk and is likely to suffer losses.

Since models form an important part of risk management, but may be characterized by simplifying or unrealistic assumptions, they must be considered and applied with care. This concept is so important that it forms one of the "cardinal rules."

5.5 IT IS IMPORTANT TO KNOW WHICH RISKS ARE MARKED-TO-MODEL AND WHY

Certain deals, products or instruments — such as complex or long-dated derivatives — are so unique and customized that they are effectively illiquid; they may, in fact, be one of a handful in the market (designed, in most cases, to meet specific client requirements). Illiquid positions generally cannot be valued using transparent prices from exchanges or pricing services, since insufficient volume exists to provide rational two-way market levels. In such cases, it is common practice to follow a "mark-to-model" procedure — essentially, valuation through a model — to generate an estimate of value. Whenever mark-to-model procedures apply, the caveats related to the underlying model assumptions mentioned above remain in force. Risk officers should be familiar with all products that are marked-to-model (rather than market, or exchange, prices), and work with financial officers and traders to ensure that the underlying risk sensitivities generated by marked-to-model procedures are as conservative and accurate as possible. It is also important for risk officers to stress the movement of risk sensitivities under various scenarios and be vigilant to large divergences or unreasonable results. Since the validity of a mark-to-model valuation can only be demonstrated over time, the establishment of protective reserves related to the amount of risk being run is generally prudent. For instance, if a bank manages a portfolio of long-dated currency options, including some with exotic features, it may be unable to get consistent market pricing to value the portfolio; the risk officer, trading manager and financial controller may thus agree to create sub-portfolios that can be valued on a mark-to-model basis. Once the sub-portfolios are identified, and the specifics of the market model independently analyzed and approved, the controller may wish to take the precautionary step of establishing a model reserve equal to a certain percentage of all outstanding transactions or some representative risk parameter. Such a reserve may be released as transactions mature, or as they are switched to a mark-to-market approach (which is likely to occur once transaction maturities reach the liquid part of the market).

5.6 THE EFFECTS OF VOLATILITY ON RISK EXPOSURES SHOULD BE QUANTIFIED

Volatility estimation is central to pricing and management of many market and credit risks, including VAR, market risk sensitivities, future credit exposure and other risk measures. As one of the key inputs to virtually every option and derivative trading/pricing model, its impact on financial results is often significant and must be considered carefully. Estimating volatility can be a very complex exercise. Various approaches may be used, including examination of historical and market-implied volatilities; this may be acceptable for generic and liquid structures, those struck near-the-money or those that are relatively short-term in nature. For structures that are farther out-of-the-money, based on unstable or gapping markets, or long-dated, historical/implied approaches may not always be adequate; using volatility forecasting techniques and stress testing volatility risk parameters can be useful in such cases. Regardless of the specific technique used, volatility estimation should be approached with prudence. In addition to using conservative estimates, firms may choose to establish volatility risk reserves to take account of discrepancies that might appear over time (with the caveat that reserves be driven by objective formulas, as we note at greater length in Chapter 7). Volatility estimates are vital but estimation techniques are not perfect; a conservative approach is therefore the best way of dealing with known shortcomings.

5.7 THE IMPACT OF CORRELATION BETWEEN ASSETS, AND BETWEEN ASSETS AND COUNTERPARTIES, SHOULD BE QUANTIFIED

Correlations, which quantify linkages between different markets, asset classes and counterparties, are a key component of many pricing, valuation and risk models. Correlations help determine how much a risk might be worth, or how an exposure might be managed within a portfolio. Though widely used, care must be taken when implementing correlations in any trading, business or risk process as they can become unstable in the presence of financial stress; instability can impact valuations, risk profiles and decision-making. For instance, a corporate bond may have an historical correlation of 0.7 versus a government bond; that is, for a unit move in the government bond, the corporate bond moves in the same direction by 70% of a unit. Knowing this, a trader may hedge a corporate bond position with a correlation-driven amount of government bonds. During times of market stress, however, the 0.7 historical correlation may no longer hold true — it may weaken to 0.2 or 0.3, or become negatively correlated as the market sells corporate bonds in favor of government bonds (in a "flight to quality"). Thus, the correlation of 0.7 that the trader utilized to hedge the bond may now be –0.4, meaning that the risk position has actually increased. The same might apply, on a broader scale, to an entire portfolio of assets and risks. Since certain market measures, such as VAR, rely on an entire matrix of cross-asset correlations (generally computed on an historical basis), a market dislocation can cause the correlation structure to break down, revealing a very different risk profile. The same can exist between markets and counterparties. While a diversified book of credit exposures (across products, markets and maturities) with a single counterparty is likely to be uncorrelated (meaning that market moves in one or more underlying markets generating credit exposure will not lead to an incidence of default), the same is not necessarily true when a counterparty has a large, concentrated and leveraged position in one or two markets — in this case the correlation between market moves and resulting exposure may be very high (and may eventually lead to default).

Since correlations can become unstable and radically skew a firm's risk profile, it is important for risk officers and business managers to stress the correlations impacting each business line. For instance, they should alter the magnitude, and direction, of the correlations underpinning pricing and risk management algorithms, and quantify how risk exposures and P&L change. Knowing the effects of financial stress on correlations, they can then determine whether to take some preventive measure, such as establishing reserves, purchasing deep out-of-the-money options, or lowering exposures.

5.8 THE VALUATION OF LARGE POSITIONS SHOULD BE REGARDED WITH SKEPTICISM; PROOF, THROUGH PERIODIC, RANDOM LIQUIDATION EXERCISES, CAN HELP PROVIDE AN ASSESSMENT OF FAIR VALUE

The valuation of large positions in securities, loans, derivatives or other financial assets must be treated conservatively, as sheer size may be sufficient to create large P&L swings in the event of rapid or forced liquidation. In general, a firm that holds a large position in a given risk (either in relation to total issue/market size or in comparison with what might be regarded as "standard") should not value the risk at the level posted on an exchange/pricing service (which is generally intended to reflect pricing for "smaller" size); risk officers should be skeptical of such a practice and work with traders and controllers to establish more realistic benchmarks. In order to establish benchmark values it is helpful to conduct periodic, random liquidation of select positions/risks — perhaps 10–20% of the total held in any given position. Though this requires a rebalancing of risk, it provides very valuable information related to the potential clearing price of the risk position. A random liquidation procedure also notifies those running large positions that they may be required to sell a piece of their portfolio at any time — this can help ensure even greater discipline in risk valuation. For example, if a market maker in corporate bonds has significant positions in three different industrial credits, the risk manager and controller may require the sale of 10% of one position over a 24-hour period. If the bond sells near the current valuation level, the mark-to-market level for the remainder of the position may be acceptable. If the bond sells more than a few points below the mark, the risk manager and controller may decide to lower the value of the entire position to the new clearing level; this will result in an immediate loss on the position, but bring it closer to "reality."

5.9 USE OF TRADITIONAL RISK QUANTIFICATION TECHNIQUES MAY UNDERESTIMATE POTENTIAL MARKET RISK LOSSES IF A PORTFOLIO OR BUSINESS IS VERY ILLIQUID

The potential market risk losses that might be sustained by a risk-taking operation that is active in illiquid positions (e.g. cash instruments that trade infrequently, long-dated/esoteric derivative risks that cannot be replicated with ease in the marketplace, and so on) may not be accurately reflected by standard risk measures. In such cases alternate metrics, which take account of illiquidity, should be employed. By adjusting a measure to reflect illiquidity, a firm is effectively scaling up its potential loss exposures and providing a more realistic assessment of what might happen in the event of forced liquidation or cover. For instance, if a firm normally computes its VAR based on a one-day holding period and a 99% confidence level, it may be severely understating its risk if its portfolio is very illiquid; in such cases it may wish to use an alternate holding period based on 10, 20, 30 or more days — any period that more closely matches the liquidity characteristics of its portfolio. For an entire business, it may wish to apply different holding periods and create a more realistic "liquidity-adjusted" VAR (LAVAR). This concept is so important that regulators have actively encouraged risk-taking institutions to develop LAVAR-related processes. The same concept applies to other estimates of risk exposure.

5.10 SCENARIO ANALYSIS CAN BE USEFUL IN QUANTIFYING HOW RISK PROFILES CHANGE WITH FLUCTUATING VARIABLES

Scenario analysis has become an integral part of the risk management process at many firms. The ability to determine how P&L and risk sensitivities change as underlying market variables move is a powerful tool that can give risk officers, business managers and senior managers a better appreciation of changing risk dynamics. Analyses that can move variables in multiple dimensions (e.g. a movement in the underlying price of an asset combined with movement in the volatility of the asset) provide a particularly interesting depiction of what can happen in volatile, rapidly changing markets. For instance, a risk officer responsible for a firm's currency exposures might apply standard scenarios that reflect a range of market moves in underlying spot prices and volatility levels; the combination allows the officer to be aware of how the firm's profitability and risk positions fare if Japanese yen appreciates by 5% and volatility rises by 10% (on a relative basis), or if the Euro depreciates by 2% and volatility remains stable. For emerging market currencies the risk officer might examine even larger market moves (approaching the "disaster scenarios" noted below). Such currency scenarios can reveal interesting portfolio risk dynamics. However, scenarios must only be regarded as a tool in the risk process, and should not be used to automatically generate or shape risk; making important risk decisions solely on the basis of scenarios may be placing too much reliance on the analytic process. As with other models, scenarios are based on assumptions about how markets and underlying variables behave; these may, or may not, be completely accurate and, as such, care must be taken when interpreting the results. In the example above, for instance, it may be unrealistic to apply small market shocks to pegged currencies (such as the Hong Kong dollar), simply because volatility has historically been low — this might result in an understatement of risk and lead to flawed risk decisions. Taken as a tool within a larger "toolbox," scenarios can be useful and informative; using them as the basis of risk decisions may lead to false comfort.

5.11 QUANTIFYING THE EFFECT OF "DISASTER" SCENARIOS ON RISK PORTFOLIOS IS USEFUL, BUT MANAGING TO SUCH SCENARIOS IS NOT AN ADVISABLE PRACTICE

It is very informative to run disaster scenarios to understand how portfolios of credit and market risks might be impacted by large market dislocations. Disaster scenarios can be defined as those with a very low probability of occurrence — a 10, 20 or 30 standard deviation event that might only be expected to occur once every few thousand years (depending on the underlying distribution used). Such scenarios can provide insight into how much a portfolio might lose or gain during extreme market turmoil — the type that has been in evidence with some frequency over the past decade. Managing a business to such scenarios, however, is not necessarily advisable. By doing so, a firm exposes itself to at least two major problems: granting too much risk capacity if it believes that the disaster scenario is unlikely to happen (because of the low probability), or granting too little risk capacity if it believes that the disaster scenario is very likely to happen (despite the seemingly low probability). For instance, if a firm runs disaster scenarios for its emerging market risk exposures, it may find that it loses a large amount of money if prices decline by 50% or currencies devalue by 50%. Not necessarily believing that these scenarios will occur (and believing that the firm is being properly compensated for the risk being assumed), the risk committee may grant risk authorization to run such positions. If the scenario is actually realized, the firm may lose more money than it thought probable; though it quantified the "worst case" downside scenario, it did not believe it would occur and accepted the risk exposure. In fact, it is often best to use disaster scenarios as an informational tool; scenarios can supplement risk limits that are based on more probable events and place an outer limit on risk capital allocation. They can also be used as a mechanism for communicating with senior managers. For instance, creating "real life" disaster scenarios based on actual events (e.g. the October 1987 crash, the 1994 Mexican peso crisis, the 1998 Russian and hedge fund crisis) helps frame the discussion in the minds of senior managers, as it lets them point to dislocations that have actually taken place.

5.12 "SAFE" ASSETS AND EXPOSURES CAN BECOME RISKY IN A CRISIS — QUANTIFYING THE DOWNSIDE OF SUCH EXPOSURES IS USEFUL

During the quantification process, a considerable effort goes into understanding how large, complex, illiquid or risky positions might be affected by a deteriorating market. This should certainly be the primary focus of attention, as it is the scenario most likely to occur. Even modest market moves can cause financial losses if positions are very large, illiquid or inherently risky (e.g. high yield or emerging market bonds). However, past events have demonstrated the advisability of quantifying the downside risk of supposedly "safe haven" assets; during a turmoil market risk positions that might normally be considered "safe" can deteriorate rapidly. For instance, during the 1998 crisis even high-rated corporate bonds (e.g. AAA/AA) suffered declines that were well in excess of what would have been expected by even the most conservative risk managers. The same can also impact credit exposures. While credit deterioration in the mid-ranges is generally quite apparent well in advance of any real problems, difficulties with investment grade credits can appear rapidly, bringing on extreme spread widening and, in some cases, default or impairment. The case of Enron, a BBB+-rated investment grade credit, emerges as an important example; over a period of less than six weeks the company announced losses, reduced its equity base, brought debt back on its balance sheet, disclosed accounting irregularities, saw its investment grade rating withdrawn and a potential "life saving" merger collapse; a liquidity crisis ensued, forcing the company to file for Chapter 11 bankruptcy protection. Thus, knowing how supposedly "safe risk" on a firm's books might behave in bad times is an important dimension of the quantification phase.

5.13 CREDIT AND MARKET RISK LINKAGES SHOULD BE QUANTIFIED WHEN POSSIBLE

In Chapter 4 we noted the importance of identifying linkages between credit and market risks; since the two can merge during times of market stress, advance identification and quantification can lead to the establishment of proactive "safety" measures. Determining the impact of correlated credit and market exposures, and how they might change under stressed market conditions, can lead to important risk management decisions — such as limiting exposures, calling for additional collateral, or avoiding business altogether. For instance, if a large, leveraged institution is known to have a very significant position in an illiquid emerging market derivative, and the potential for counterparty default is high, then the impact of default on the underlying derivative market should be estimated, since other institutions may be covering the position at the same time — possibly moving the market and creating even greater losses. Alternatively, if an obligor defaults on a liability that serves as a derivative reference index, an estimate of how that risk event might impact counterparty credit exposures should be undertaken. During the Russian crisis of 1998 a moratorium by Russia on its rouble denominated debt (including GKO treasury securities) led to a large increase in credit exposure to funds that had transacted GKO/rouble "carry" trades. As the value of the GKOs and rouble plummeted, credit exposures to funds increased, margin calls were made by banks extending credit, and funds were forced to liquidate assets and collateral to meet the calls — in some cases to the point of failure; the correlation between the performance of Russian GKOs and the funds as counterparties to GKO trades was extremely high — advance quantification of such linkages can help minimize financial losses.

5.14 LEVERAGE CAN MAGNIFY CREDIT, MARKET, FUNDING AND LIQUIDITY RISKS AND MUST BE FACTORED INTO ANY QUANTIFICATION EXERCISE

Earlier we indicated that the use of leverage should be identified in any counterparty relationship or product structure, as the effects of excessive leverage can increase credit, market, funding and asset liquidity risks. Measurement techniques used to quantify risk exposures need to be calibrated to take account of leverage. Failure to do so may result in mismanagement of the risk portfolio and lead to excess losses, particularly during market dislocations when illiquidity, price gapping and counterparty deterioration appear. This applies to both market and credit risks. For instance, if a firm uses VAR to compute the risk of a highly leveraged portfolio, it might choose a more conservative liquidation period or implement broader LAVAR measurement techniques. Alternatively, if the firm is extending credit to a leveraged counterparty by taking corporate bonds as collateral, it may wish to take an excess amount of collateral to compensate for any difficulties in liquidating bonds following counterparty default. The quantitative process can help crystallize incremental exposures that might become evident through leverage.

5.15 RELYING ON A MARK-TO-MARKET CALCULATION AS AN ESTIMATE OF REPLACEMENT COST AT THE TIME OF DEFAULT MIGHT RESULT IN AN UNDERSTATEMENT

Market stress situations can render standard estimates of replacement cost, such as normal mark-to-market valuation, insufficient. This is particularly true when the underlying market is illiquid, collateral being held to secure exposures is unsaleable, and/or a counterparty is highly leveraged or concentrated. These factors can result in an understatement of exposure and, in the event of default, a greater than expected loss. Any measure of replacement cost (or current exposure) must be conservative enough to capture the effects of a stressed environment, which might include volatility, price gapping, illiquidity and excess leverage. For instance, a conservative measure of replacement cost might focus on the liquidation, or buy-in, value of a position based on stressed, rather than normal, market conditions. If a firm believes that its replacement cost to a given counterparty is $5MM under normal circumstances, it may wish to increment that amount by a factor that reflects the underlying drivers of the exposure. By quantifying scenarios it may determine that a more appropriate liquidation value is in the range of $8–10MM. If a firm needs to replace its contract with a defaulting counterparty in a market that is very illiquid and prone to price gapping, its replacement cost should be adjusted upward to reflect those characteristics.

5.16 QUANTIFYING CREDIT EXPOSURES ON A NET BASIS SHOULD ONLY BE DONE WHEN A FIRM HAS APPROPRIATE COUNTERPARTY DOCUMENTATION AND IS OPERATING IN A JURISDICTION WHERE NETTING IS LEGALLY RECOGNIZED

Through the efforts of financial and legal practitioners, and regulators, the netting of credit exposures has taken greater hold in the financial system. Under a netting scheme a portfolio of trades with a single counterparty governed by a master agreement can be condensed into a single payment or receipt in the event of counterparty default. As a result, creditors no longer have to worry about a bankruptcy administrator honoring trades that favor the bankrupt client, while dismissing those that penalize the client (a concept known as "cherry picking"). In order for netting to be used with confidence, the legal validity of the master agreement must be accepted in the relevant jurisdiction. For instance, the concept of netting is permissible in the US, the UK, select parts of Continental Europe and Japan, among others. This allows firms to quantify and manage credit risk exposures on a net basis, rather than assuming a "worst case" cherry-picking scenario. Once again, this only applies in instances where a valid netting agreement exists between two parties; netting cannot occur if there is no agreement. If a bank has a portfolio of derivatives with a counterparty that is covered by an ISDA master agreement, and the governing law covering the agreement is US-based, quantification of credit exposures with that counterparty can be done on a net basis. In countries where netting has not been recognized, or where there is concern regarding the lack of case law supporting netting, care must be taken when considering net versus gross credit exposures. A prudent firm is likely to opt for a more conservative approach, which is to assume that any trades with value will be dismissed in the event of counterparty default. Knowing this, it will quantify its exposure on a gross basis and conduct its credit decision-making in a more conservative fashion.

5.17 THE EFFICACY OF RISK ANALYTICS SHOULD BE DEMONSTRATED THROUGH REGULAR QUANTITATIVE TESTING

In order to determine whether risk analytics, including instrument pricing tools, portfolio risk aggregators, VAR processes, and so forth, are performing as expected (given the assumptions underpinning the analytics), it is useful to engage in regular testing of results. Testing can be done against risk sensitivities generated by particular pricing formulas as well as the P&L function (meaning that the ability to decompose and explain P&L, as discussed in Chapter 6, is an essential requirement). Testing generally involves comparing actual results against those produced by an analytic process. If a significant variation appears between what is expected and what is actually achieved, further enhancements in the analytics are almost certain to be required; diagnosis of the problem should be undertaken until the source of the discrepancy is located. Testing of results is receiving greater scrutiny from regulators, particularly as related to VAR processes. Most regulators recommend a regular regimen of "backtesting" in order to confirm the validity of a firm's VAR process. For instance, a firm implementing a new VAR process may wish to compare the results of each day's VAR against those actually realized through the daily P&L revaluation process. Over an extended period of time — perhaps six to 12 months — the firm will begin to gain experience with the new process and how it compares to actual results; it may then accept the results or seek to enhance its process. It is good practice to document results and make them available to others in the governance and control structure.

5.18 INDEPENDENT VERIFICATION OF THE ANALYTICS USED TO QUANTIFY RISKS SHOULD BE UNDERTAKEN

Since trading, valuation and risk analytics form a central part of the business operations of any risk-bearing firm, it is important that tools used to price, trade and manage risk be as accurate and correct as possible. Since no model is perfect, and most require users to make certain assumptions, it is worth verifying that they are mathematically sound. In order to avoid any potential "conflict of interest," and to preserve the independence that is so important in the risk governance framework, analytics should be reviewed by independent experts. Large firms with significant risk resources may assign dedicated quantitative experts from the risk management function to review the mathematical work developed by other business-based quantitative specialists. In smaller organizations, the function may have to be outsourced to third-party consultants or auditors with appropriate technical skills. Regardless of how the analytics are reviewed, results should be discussed and documented; if flaws or errors are discovered, a program of corrective action should be undertaken. Summary results of model reviews should be communicated to the risk committee and others in the governance structure; since model risk is a source of exposure to any firm using analytics, those ultimately responsible for approving firm-wide risk resources should be kept apprised of findings and potential risks. The review process should be continuous. Since analytics change as markets shift or new products are added, the risk control function must establish a regular regimen of model review. For instance, if a firm active in equity derivative trading uses a variety of models and algorithms to price and hedge its equity derivative book, the underlying financial mathematics used to create the models must be analyzed and tested by the independent risk function. If, at the conclusion of the analysis process, the review indicates that nine of 10 models are mathematically sound but one requires enhancements, the risk specialist may recommend the establishment of a model reserve until the shortcoming is resolved. As part of the review, the documented results and recommendation may be presented to the risk committee and filed for later use by internal or external auditors and regulators.

Summarizing the simple rules related to the quantification process, we note the following:

- All risks flagged during the identification stage should be decomposed and quantified — this assigns value to risk, and permits subsequent limiting, monitoring and managing.
- Since the quantification process introduces extensive use of financial mathematics and assumptions, care must be taken to understand potential shortcomings and the existence of model risk.
- The presence of model risk suggests that the results generated by analytic processes should not be relied on to the point of "blind faith;" models are tools that supplement, rather than replace, aspects of the risk management function — they should not be the sole source of a firm's risk decision-making process.

- When examining market, credit and liquidity exposures, care must be taken to quantify the effects of correlation, volatility and liquidity on valuation; quantifying known linkages between credit and market risks should also be undertaken — adjustments, in the form of conservative pricing or the establishment of reserves, should always be considered.
- Scenario analysis, like other pricing and management algorithms, should be used to quantify the effects of small and large market movements on portfolios of risks; however, results should be interpreted and used in a proper context.
- Since the quantitative process is such an important part of risk management, results that are generated by models should be compared against results actually achieved; this can reveal the efficacy or shortcomings of given models.
- All quantitative processes should, of course, be reviewed and tested independently, to ensure that no model errors exist and that underlying assumptions are properly vetted.

6 Risk Monitoring and Reporting

Monitoring and reporting of risk constitutes the verification and communication stage of the risk management process. Monitoring, which involves internal scrutiny and tracking of exposures in relation to limits/policies, and reporting, which centers on internal and external communication of exposures, are essential in any risk-taking firm. Detailed monitoring and reporting typically occurs within the risk management function itself, between risk management and business units, and between risk management and those in the governance structure; summary reporting is generally used as a link to outside parties, including regulators, credit rating agencies, bank lenders (and other credit providers) and shareholders. Risk reporting is often the most "visible" aspect of the risk process. Though identifying, defining, quantifying and managing risks are key elements of the process, they are largely invisible to those who are not directly involved. Reporting, in contrast, is the primary mechanism by which information is communicated, and by which internal and external parties gain an understanding of a firm's risk profile and its overall risk process; it therefore constitutes a visible, and vital, link in the overall risk framework.

6.1 IF RISK CANNOT BE MONITORED IT CANNOT BE MANAGED

Any firm that intends to take, and manage, risk must be able to monitor its exposures. Though this may seem simple and logical, it is often a very complex process — particularly in large firms that manage risk across multiple products, markets and regions. If a business unit cannot monitor the risk it intends to take, it may ultimately sustain losses as a result of its inability to accurately recognize and manage its exposures; others in the governance structure will be equally "blind" to current exposures, and regulators will not receive a true picture of the firm's consolidated risk. For example, if a firm active in interest rate derivatives decides to create a new derivative structure that cannot be accommodated in the current technology platform — and which must, therefore, be housed in a manually intensive spreadsheet that is incapable of generating risk reporting — it cannot monitor its risk effectively and is unlikely to be in full control of its exposures. Until an audited spreadsheet platform or the firm's standard technology platform can accommodate the new derivative product and report on its risks, the trader should not participate in the market. Only when risk can be reported in sufficient granularity to allow proper management can a firm be truly aware of its risk exposures.

6.2 TOP RISKS SHOULD BE MONITORED CONTINUOUSLY

Identifying and monitoring select risk exposures that have the potential of creating significant losses for a firm is a worthwhile practice. Institutions often have pockets of risk that are heavily influenced by the movement of select markets or the performance of particular counterparties. Though firms actively diversify their risk as part of the overall risk management processes, specializations in markets or counterparties can appear — this results in mild concentration risks. Knowing this, it is useful for risk officers to identify the five to 10 markets and counterparties that generate the majority of the firm's risk. Regular communication of these variables and exposures to senior managers, risk committee members and directors is good practice, as it permits immediate awareness on whether a particular market or credit event is likely to create financial problems for the firm. Once these key risk variables have been identified, risk officers should monitor them for warning signs (e.g. widening of spreads, rise in volatility, deterioration in counterparty credit, and so on) and take action when necessary. For instance, a firm might be most heavily exposed to US credit spreads, US interest rates, European equity volatility and Latin-bloc currencies; it may also have significant credit exposures to Companies A, B and C, and convertibility risk in Brazil. Knowing that these risks can have a significant impact on the firm, the risk group may prepare a specific daily report that updates others in the business units and governance structure on the status and performance of each exposure.

6.3 THE USE OF A "RISK WATCHLIST" REPORT, WHICH ALERTS PARTICIPANTS TO POTENTIAL CONCERNS OR PROBLEM AREAS, CAN BE A VALUABLE MANAGEMENT TOOL

Though all credit, market, legal and operational risks need to be reported on a regular basis, it is often helpful to isolate the problem areas that a risk function is most concerned about, and report on them through a separate "risk watchlist" — these need not necessarily be a firm's top risks, but those it is especially concerned about. Distributing a risk watchlist to business and control units acquaints a broader audience with problem counterparties, market risk positions, documentary backlogs, settlement problems, and so on; sensitizing others to potential problem areas improves monitoring capabilities (i.e. more individuals will be watching for warning signs), and may permit the firm to take protective actions when needed. For example, a credit function might have unsecured credit exposures with 10 sub-investment grade counterparties that it is concerned about and might circulate this credit watchlist to business, finance and operations professionals every week. A trader, aware from the marketplace of potential difficulties with one of the counterparties on the watchlist, may contact the credit officer with the news; the credit officer and trader, after discussion, may elect to purchase default protection on the counterparty to protect the outstanding exposure.

6.4 STANDARD RISK REPORTS SHOULD BE SUPPLEMENTED BY SPECIAL REPORTS THAT PROVIDE AN INDICATION OF ILLIQUIDITY, MISMARKS AND OTHER PROBLEMS

In addition to standard risk reports that detail a firm's top risks, its exposure to counterparties, market variables (e.g. direction, volatility, correlation), concentrations, and so on, numerous other "early warning" reporting mechanisms can be designed to permit monitoring of problem positions. For instance, reports that measure the turnover occurring on a particular desk can illustrate whether flows have strengthened or weakened over some predefined reporting period. If a business manager notes that the normal volume of trades flowing through a desk is weaker than usual, it may indicate several potential problems: lack of focus by the sales force on the product; bad pricing by the trading desk; or broader market turmoil which forces all players to curtail activity. If the trading involves the extension of credit (e.g. a forward settling or swap transaction), it may also be indicative of actual or perceived credit problems with the firm itself. A turnover measure can thus provide business and trading managers with important early warning signs that can prompt defensive actions (e.g. a gradual lowering of positions or the construction of an appropriate hedge). Similar information can be obtained from aged position reports, which reflect the number and size of risk positions that are selling very slowly (or not at all). For instance, if a firm has underwritten a corporate bond issue at a level that it believes will clear the market but finds that two months later it is left with the same position, it may have been too aggressive in its pricing; the aged inventory report tracking any position on the book over 60 or 90 days can be a useful tool for controllers, helping them verify valuations on aged positions. If an issue has not sold over 60 or 90 days, the controller may wish to examine the carrying price and mark down accordingly. Such reports can also be a good indicator of willful misvaluation of a book or position, and should become part of the overall reporting and monitoring effort.

6.5 IT IS MORE USEFUL TO HAVE TIMELY REPORTING OF 90% OF A FIRM'S RISK EXPOSURE THAN DELAYED REPORTING OF 100%

While a 100% picture of risk, on a near real time basis, is the ideal reporting goal for many institutions, it is very difficult to capture every risk instantaneously and accurately in a complex and fast-moving environment. While small, mono-line firms might be able to identify their credit, market and liquidity risks in real time (and extend the platform to identify legal and settlement risks), any firm with scale or multi-product focus is likely to have a very difficult time capturing all of its risks within hours of closing its books. Most large firms operate multiple trading/business, middle-office and back-end platforms, that may, or may not, communicate effectively. In the absence of robust technical links, alternate risk aggregation methods may be required — and could result in time delays. Accordingly, a realistic, but still prudent, reporting approach might target 90% of exposures that can be compiled quickly, followed by the remainder the next morning. The availability of timely risk information that covers the bulk of a firm's risk should generally be sufficient for short-term decision-making. It is often more important to deliver a near real time picture of the majority of the firm's risk than a complete profile on a delayed basis (e.g. the following day) — by which time some exposures will have begun to change. Naturally, institutions that have a platform capable of delivering complete, accurate, end-of-day risk information are positioned to lead the industry in this area; for firms that have not yet attained such capabilities it is a worthwhile goal — as long as the costs are not prohibitive. In the interim, a process that captures the bulk of a firm's exposure in a timely fashion is an acceptable compromise.

6.6 INFORMATION SHOULD NOT COME FROM MULTIPLE SOURCES — A SINGLE, INDEPENDENT SOURCE SHOULD BE USED AS THE KERNEL FOR ALL REPORTS, AND SHOULD BE AUDITED FOR ACCURACY ON A REGULAR BASIS

Since accurate, reliable risk information is the essence of sound monitoring and reporting, risk officers, business managers and others in the governance structure must be able to refer, with confidence, to the information they are receiving. This can only be done if risk information for a business (or entire groups of businesses) comes from a single source. In essence, the trading blotter that comprises a business unit's record of trades must feed into all middle- and back-office processes and become the sole source of information for risk management purposes; this should also include information required for reconciliation of books and records and the creation of the P&L function. Thus, a fixed income trading desk's system should be the source of market and credit risk reports, P&L, operational breaks, legal backlog, and so forth. Risk information that resides outside of the official trading system (e.g. pending trades, exotic structures that do not fit within the confines of the system, and so on) results in the need for multiple feeds into a platform which produces risk reports; this means discrepancies can arise and manual reconciliation processes must be utilized. Over the medium-term this can lead to corrupt data and inaccuracies. It should be the priority of any risk-taking organization to centralize all information for a business in a single platform so that users can have confidence in the material they are reviewing; over the medium and long-term, all businesses should be accommodated in the same platform (or in distinct platforms that feature seamless functionality and communication).

6.7 THE ABILITY TO RELATE PROFIT AND LOSS TO RISK, IN DETAIL, IS PARAMOUNT

Understanding the ultimate source of profits and losses, and relating this back to risk exposure, is an essential component of risk management. Monitoring risk, and the profit and loss effects of risk, must always be done jointly; a risk process is only effective when it controls risk, and the only way of being certain that it is being controlled is by examining its impact on P&L. Market and credit risks are assumed in order to generate profits; as discussed in Chapter 2, a proper financial intermediation process prices risk into all transactions and businesses. It is therefore vital to trace the impact of risk on profits — this helps determine whether the risk being assumed is producing the returns expected, and whether analytics used to produce risk measures are accurate. Explaining how profits and losses arise is thus a central requirement of any risk process.

The "P&L explain" process, as it is often called, is not usually simple to implement in a firm with multiple business lines and a broad range of risks; however, since it is a vital part of best practice and regulatory risk management, it is worth the time, cost and effort. The process must be able to distinguish, with sufficient precision, how money is made and lost. Revenue sources must be decomposed into individual categories, including fees, commissions, interest, new deal revenue, trading gains, and so on; within each of these broad categories, various detailed sub-categories should be explored. For instance, trading gains might be decomposed into intraday and hold positions; hold position revenues might then be segregated into various additional "risk classes," including direction, volatility, time decay, basis, curve shift, and so on. The ultimate goal is to be able to refer to a given risk and understand its contribution to the firm's profitability. This provides an understanding of how the firm makes and loses money, permits effective allocation of resources (under a risk-adjusted performance framework, for example), and serves as an important validation tool for the VAR process. It also gives management important insight into how the firm, and individual businesses and traders, take and manage risk.

Being able to explain how risk positions impact a firm's profits and losses is so vital that it forms one of the "cardinal rules."

6.8 PROFITS MUST BE REVIEWED WITH THE SAME RIGOR AS LOSSES AS THEY MAY BE INDICATIVE OF LARGE, OR UNKNOWN, RISKS

When a firm sustains a financial loss, managers typically demand detailed explanations; large losses require even more detailed explanations — indeed, they are virtually guaranteed to generate formal internal control and audit investigations. This is an understandable, and logical, process — especially if lessons can be learned about how, and why, the losses occurred. It is imperative, however, that the same discipline be applied when the firm is making a great deal of money, as the same forces that cause losses — model error, mismarking, excess risk, market volatility, and so on — may be at work. Unfortunately, this often fails to happen. Managers are rewarded for generating revenues — the larger the revenues, the greater the praise and financial reward. When revenues are being generated, there is typically little incentive or pressure to analyze how they are being created. This can lead to false comfort and may mask underlying problems or difficulties that only become known once market circumstances turn against the firm; by then it may be too late to avoid large losses. Indeed, it is possible that all of the revenues generated in seemingly "good" times will be given up during a short market dislocation. For instance, many financial firms profited handsomely from "carry trades" in Mexico, Brazil and other emerging markets in the 1990s — booking large profits and receiving support from management in the form of additional risk capital. When the currency crises hit the emerging markets in 1994, 1997 and 1998, many of the same firms lost considerable amounts of money on once-profitable risk positions. This was probably not a surprise to the small number of firms capable of explaining their P&L in good, as well as bad, times but it was certainly a shock to those who had "forgotten" about profits reaped before the dislocations occurred. Profits must always be questioned as thoroughly as losses, and the best way of doing so is through a rigorous P&L explain mechanism.

6.9 SOME RISK POSITIONS GENERATE LOSSES INSTANTANEOUSLY WHILE OTHERS BLEED PROFITS OVER TIME; P&L DECOMPOSITION CAN HELP IDENTIFY LOSSES IN BOTH CASES

A powerful attribute of a fully-functioning P&L explain process is its ability to help identify risk positions that create small losses over a long period of time. While sudden and significant losses — from large market moves, or a major counterparty default — are simple to identify, smaller losses may prove frustrating to locate — and may ultimately cost as much as a single large loss. For instance, a very complex derivatives book, with thousands of positions that are valued through a variety of models, may be the source of very subtle P&L changes over a long period of time. In absence of a mechanism to explain the source of P&L, a team of controllers might spend a considerable amount of time dissecting the portfolio, running it through scenarios, tracking performance and reconciling positions, in order to determine the reason for the losses; even after going through such efforts it might be difficult to ascertain whether the problem has been uncovered. An effective P&L explain process can help track the source of profit drains and allow business managers to readjust their positions, fix pricing algorithms, create defensive hedges, or take other protective actions.

6.10 REPORTING SHOULD FOCUS ON THE ESSENTIAL — SIMPLE REPORTS THAT CONVEY THE RIGHT INFORMATION ARE OFTEN THE MOST EFFECTIVE TOOL

In an age where significant amounts of information are readily available there is a temptation to deluge business managers, senior managers and risk committee members with as much detailed risk and finance information as possible. This can be overwhelming and counterproductive. Effective risk reporting — certainly at the senior/executive management level — should be based on simple and straightforward information. Reporting should be detailed enough to describe the firm's risk profile but succinct enough to be digestible. In addition, reports should be free of jargon and "trader-speak;" senior managers should not be required to review and interpret reports that convey risk in terms intended primarily for traders or bankers. The risk management or control function responsible for creating management information should communicate essential items in clear, universally understood, terms.

6.11 MANAGEMENT REPORTING SHOULD GENERALLY COMMENCE WITH BROAD SUMMARIES OF KEY RISKS FOR BOARD DIRECTORS AND SENIOR EXECUTIVES, AND INCREASE IN DETAIL AS IT MOVES DOWN THE MANAGEMENT CHAIN

Delivering the right information to the right people, at the right time, is a vital dimension of proper risk management. A board member should not receive a 50 page report every day listing a counterparty's detailed credit portfolio, or a 25 page report noting equity derivative positions — the detail is irrelevant to the board member's oversight function and likely to be a waste of time and resources. Likewise, providing a complex FX options trader or a treasury manager with a weekly summary report of counterparty, market and liquidity risks is ineffective — the report is unlikely to contain enough information, or be supplied frequently enough, for business leaders to make reasoned risk decisions. Information must be tailored to the needs of the audience and delivered according to a schedule that allows for proper review and action. Thus, board members should receive weekly or monthly summary risk reports that allow them to discharge their fiduciary responsibilities in an effective manner while trading and business managers should receive daily risk reports with enough counterparty and market risk information to allow them to make trading and credit decisions. Business managers, senior managers and risk committee members should receive some hybrid of the two — perhaps daily summary reports and a weekly detailed report, or some other combination that allows them to perform their own management and oversight functions.

6.12 SENIOR MANAGERS IN THE RISK GOVERNANCE STRUCTURE MUST RECEIVE AND REVIEW RISK INFORMATION ON A REGULAR BASIS

In Chapter 3 we discussed the importance of implementing a proper risk governance structure; a key part of any governance process is communication. In order for the structure to be effective, executives that comprise the structure — senior executives, board members, risk committee members, and so on — must review risk information on a regular basis. By reviewing reports that accurately reflect the firm's exposures, those in the risk governance structure become knowledgeable about, and accountable for, the firm's risk; when board members, risk committee members and senior risk officers receive information, they become aware of the firm's risk profile and help ensure it falls within the parameters of the risk mandate. It is crucial, therefore, for governance members to receive regular risk information. For instance, a bank's risk management and financial control functions might prepare a package of summary market, credit and P&L information for review and comment by the risk committee, executive management team and board; this may be supplemented by a review of risks and trends by the bank's senior risk officer. By providing regular risk information to all appropriate parties, the bank adheres to the requirements of the governance process.

6.13 READY ACCESS TO DETAILED RISK INFORMATION IS CRITICAL

Expanding on the rules above, it is important for trading and risk managers to have access to detailed risk information when needed. Though the audience for extremely detailed information is typically quite limited — primarily risk officers, traders, bankers, financial controllers and auditors — it is important for such parties to have full access to detailed records for ongoing risk review, analysis and discussion. Indeed, the risk information used by book-runners to manage their market and credit risk exposures should be accessible by managers and control officers; this helps ensure that all personnel are referring to the same source and type of information, leaving no room for discrepancies or misinterpretation. It also enhances transparency and reduces the chance that positions or risks can be "buried" in detailed trading reports. For instance, a market risk officer responsible for a firm's commodity exposure should be able to access the trading systems and trade-level risk reports that are used by the firm's commodity traders; this should provide the risk officer with visibility to all relevant risk information on trading risk in physical commodities, listed and OTC derivative contracts and structured products. If the risk officer needs to query a specific trade or position, he or she has the information to do so.

6.14 REPORTING SHOULD BE FLEXIBLE ENOUGH TO PROVIDE ALL RELEVANT VIEWS OF RISK INFORMATION

As noted earlier, participants in the business, risk management and governance processes have unique needs when it comes to risk reporting. A trader managing specific risk needs detailed information on those risks. Business and risk managers need broader aggregations of risk — across products, asset classes, markets or regions — in order to risk-manage entire businesses. Those located in regional offices require regional segregations of risk data, while those managing local legal entities need legal entity risk information. Since each one of these constituencies has very specific, and legitimate, needs for seeing risk information in a particular form, reporting must be as flexible as possible. Being able to accommodate only one or two views of risk is unlikely to be adequate for global institutions that run broad-based risk operations. For instance, if an international bank is only able to depict risk by product (e.g. US interest rate derivatives, European equities, Japanese yen spot/forward) it is unlikely to satisfy business and risk management, executive management and regulators; the bank may then have to devote additional resources to creating manual reporting mechanisms that allow for more flexible views of information. The ideal platform should deliver a full suite of risk information in any form required. As noted earlier, information must be drawn from the same underlying data source; thus, data for legal entity reporting should come from the same source as data for product management reporting, and so forth. If this does not occur, discrepancies will eventually arise and manually intensive reconciliation efforts will be required.

6.15 REGULATORY REPORTS ARE GENERALLY NOT SUFFICIENT TO MANAGE A COMPLEX BUSINESS

Global regulators require firms operating in their jurisdictions to submit regular information on credit and market risks. While these efforts are generally well intentioned and designed to provide some notion of the "macro" state of any firm's risk profile, they are inadequate to internally manage any complex business. Information prepared for most regulatory agencies is typically not granular enough to reveal important details about a firm's risk profile and is, therefore, likely to be insufficient for business management purposes. Most regulators do not require (and most institutions would be reluctant to disclose) detailed risk positions by asset class, risk factor, market or counterparty. This means that two risk reporting tracks must be followed: one for regulators and one for internal management. Though this results in extra costs and resources, the alternatives are unattractive: providing overly detailed information to regulators or providing insufficiently detailed information to business and risk managers.

6.16 REGULATORY REPORTING REQUIREMENTS ARE LIKELY TO INCREASE OVER TIME AND SHOULD BE BORNE IN MIND WHEN DESIGNING REPORTING MECHANISMS

Over the past few decades, regulators have demanded increasing amounts of risk information from institutions operating in their jurisdictions. It is likely that as global financial markets continue to expand, and become more volatile and interdependent, global regulators will seek even more information regarding risk activities; the trend towards requesting more risk information has been evident throughout the 1980s and 1990s, and there is little reason to believe that it will reverse. Accordingly, those responsible for creating risk reports should be flexible in designing and implementing reporting mechanisms. While many institutions produce regulatory reports as a "by-product" of their existing risk infrastructure (typically with delays of weeks, or even months), there is likely to be an increasing need to create mechanisms that produce customized regulatory reports over much shorter time frames; next-generation risk reporting mechanisms should incorporate this flexibility. While regulators may be satisfied with the detail and classification they are currently receiving from institutions, regulatory changes are likely to result in requests for different views or additional detail; being prepared to meet such demands through a flexible mechanism can help a firm avoid creating, or recreating, risk information at a later time.

6.17 MORE, RATHER THAN LESS, DISCLOSURE OF CREDIT AND MARKET RISKS TO EXTERNAL PARTIES IS PREFERABLE; IT ADDS TRANSPARENCY AND COMFORT

A common criticism arising during times of financial stress is the lack of transparency surrounding financial and risk information; not surprisingly, the marketplace in general, and regulators in particular, typically demand an increased level of reporting transparency in the aftermath of a crisis. For instance, following the Latin LDC crisis of the 1980s, which culminated in large reserving actions by major US and international banks, institutions became more forthcoming about their counterparty exposures, reserve allocations, non-performing assets, and so on. This behavior was reinforced by the 1988 BIS capital allocation rules, which required a predefined amount of capital to be applied to risk assets; this, again, codified the risk information that institutions were beginning to divulge voluntarily. Much the same occurred in the aftermath of the LTCM/hedge fund crisis, when funds were criticized for not providing enough financial information about their financial operations and portfolios; since most operated as offshore entities, regulators were unable to directly influence the process. As a result, many large Wall Street firms, who had extended credit to the sector, became more demanding of their hedge fund clients — insisting on greater amounts of financial transparency in order to continue doing business.

In general, the marketplace is moving toward a standard of more, rather than less, financial disclosure. This relates to market and credit risk exposures, for which there are acceptable ways of expressing information; it is also starting to relate to liquidity exposures, where firms are computing liquidity-adjusted measures (e.g. LAVAR, stressed funding, and so on). It has yet to be applied rigorously in other sectors, such as legal and operational risks, where metrics are not yet as clear or uniform. Being able to disclose as much risk information as possible, without revealing competitive details, is generally a wise course of action; internal and external stakeholders are likely to favor the transparency. Firms that are regarded as "leading edge" in their disclosure policies are generally viewed as role models for others in the industry. Those seeking to disclose as little as possible, or to obfuscate a true risk/financial picture (while still operating within the "letter of the law") may eventually run afoul of investors, clients and regulators. Enron, which attempted to alter its financial picture by moving assets and debt off-balance sheet and inflating earnings, serves as a good example of "lack of transparency." In the extreme, failure to provide relevant information to internal and external parties can lead to loss of confidence and financial stress.

6.18 REPORTING SHOULD NOT BE AIMED AT VERY LIMITED AUDIENCES OR BE DONE "FOR SHOW"

Risk reporting consumes valuable human and technological resources, particularly in large organizations that operate multiple business lines, products and locations; accordingly, it must be directed and managed wisely. In particular, risk reports should be useful, conveying information that is valuable to business and trading managers, executive managers, bankers, risk managers and regulators. Reports should not be produced "for show" or for a very limited group of users — this consumes resources while adding little, or no, incremental value. In an era where internal and external constituencies demand increasing amounts of risk information, firms must resist the temptation to produce reports that "look nice" but convey little, or that satisfy a small audience without advancing the broader interests of the business, risk process and firm.

In general, regulators have been reasonable when requesting information — they have a good understanding of the type of information needed to manage a business, and are therefore unlikely to burden firms with information requests that serve no purpose. Equally, most internal groups know which reports are useful and which are not — and are unlikely to require a business or its control group to produce those of limited value. However, risk managers and product controllers who are charged with producing independent risk reports must focus on creating only those reports that are truly useful. For example, if a particular manager wants his team members to receive regular customized reports, those in the risk function/financial control should determine whether such reports are truly necessary (or whether they can be replaced by other sources of information); customized, limited audience, resource-intensive reporting should be kept to an absolute minimum (indeed, it may be more worthwhile spending time and effort creating a flexible reporting platform than individual custom reports).

6.19 USE OF "FLASH REPORTING" CAN PROVIDE AN EARLY INDICATION OF P&L AND RISK PERFORMANCE

Risk managers and trading managers can often benefit from intraday and end-of-day "flash reporting" to provide an indication of how risk positions are impacting profitability. Flash reporting is essentially an "unofficial" estimate of P&L and risk that traders and business managers prepare based on their knowledge of the day's events — including dealing activity, risk positions, customer deals, market moves, reserving actions, and so on. For instance, if an equity desk is running a very large position in stock ABC and the trader sees the price rise by 10%, he can quickly estimate the P&L impact; during the course of the day he might add in the effects of ABC buys/sells and sales commissions and then compute an ending P&L and risk position. The rest of the equity desk can do the same for all other positions, the entire business unit can do so for all business lines, and so on. The end result is a preliminary view of risk and P&L. It should be stressed that flash reporting is unofficial; it is not intended to represent a firm's accounting books and records, as official P&L and risk can only be published once all trades have been settled and reconciled, and controllers have completed their valuation work. Despite the fact that the information is unofficial, however, it can be of enormous use to those seeking early information on how the day's P&L and risk positions will finish. Flash reporting is made possible, of course, by automation; absent the right technological infrastructure, such an exercise is likely to be too time-consuming, especially for complex businesses (such as derivatives, cross-region products, and so forth).

6.20 MONITORING PROCESSES SHOULD BE IMPLEMENTED TO VERIFY THE NATURE OF COLLATERAL AND COUNTERPARTIES

In dealing with particular types of counterparties — primarily those that are sub-investment grade, or to which a firm has already extended a large amount of credit — risk officers often require collateral to be posted as security; this permits risk-related business to proceed within prudent risk parameters. However, effective implementation of this process requires a monitoring mechanism in order to ensure proper collateral is taken. Thus, if a credit officer requires a counterparty to post US Treasuries, the process must confirm that the Treasuries specified are actually received. If business directives permit accepting collateral of lesser credit quality — say, A-rated corporate bonds of a particular maturity and industry — then a proper monitoring mechanism is even more important, since the value of the collateral can deteriorate even more rapidly. The mechanism should be able to identify any collateral that has been posted erroneously. If a credit officer indicates that five-year coupon-bearing Treasuries can be used as collateral to secure a counterparty exposure, but the counterparty forwards 30-year zero-coupon Treasuries (with much greater price volatility), the process should be able to flag the discrepancy and alert the credit officer and settlements specialist. A collateral monitoring mechanism can be implemented and overseen by the securities settlements unit, with a proper link back to the risk management function.

In a similar light, credit officers grant counterparties credit based on the fundamental creditworthiness of the actual party to a transaction; since it is important to identify the actual counterparty to a trade, a firm must create a monitoring mechanism to verify its counterparties. This process acquires a legal character as it is based on confirming that the legal counterparty to a trade is the same counterparty that has been approved by the credit officer. A legal monitoring framework, with a link back to risk management, can be effective in preventing counterparty misidentification problems. For example, if a credit officer approves a credit transaction with Company ABC Inc. based on its review and acceptance of ABC Inc. as a creditworthy entity, substitution of ABC Co. (Bermuda), an offshore subsidiary of inferior credit standing (without the benefit of parent support), should be flagged by the monitoring process and sent to legal and credit professionals for resolution. In the event that incorrect collateral is delivered or the wrong counterparty confirms a trade, immediate action must be taken to correct the problem; allowing either problem to persist can result in unsecured exposure or outright loss due to counterparty failure.

6.21 PUBLIC CREDIT RATINGS CAN BE USEFUL FOR "THIRD PARTY" CONFIRMATION AND MONITORING, BUT SHOULD NOT BE REGARDED AS A SUBSTITUTE FOR PROPRIETARY INTERNAL RATINGS

Public credit rating agencies, such as Standard and Poor's, Moody's and FitchIBCA, provide credit rating services to many companies in the marketplace — particularly, though not exclusively, to those that issue public securities. Credit officers at many firms routinely use public credit ratings in their assessment of counterparty creditworthiness. Firms tend to use public ratings in one of two forms: as the sole source of credit analysis/evaluation, or as supplementary information. Some firms cannot afford a large credit function to independently review and rate all counterparties and must therefore rely on information in the public domain; this effectively means that a portion of the credit risk process — analysis and rating — is placed in the hands of a third-party institution. While decisions related to the amount and tenor of risk exposure remain with the firm's risk officers, actual evaluation of the financial condition of the client is outsourced. If, as a result of limited resources, this is the only solution available, then it is better than having no credit process at all. However, to the extent a firm has the ability to rate its own counterparties, it should strive to do so — this permits it to apply its own criteria and philosophy in analyzing potential counterparties. In such instances reference to outside ratings can be helpful as an ancillary tool (or "second opinion"), but the firm is effectively in control of its entire risk process. Ongoing monitoring of public credit ratings is, of course, a useful exercise regardless of the model selected.

6.22 FINANCIAL MARKETS CONTAIN A GREAT DEAL OF CREDIT INFORMATION — MONITORING THE STOCK PRICES AND CREDIT SPREADS OF COUNTERPARTIES CAN BE HELPFUL, ESPECIALLY ON THE DOWNSIDE

A criticism often levied at credit officers is that they are slow to react to deteriorating credit quality; by the time a given counterparty is downgraded, the firm may already be heavily exposed to the performance of a weakening counterparty. Credit officers often view themselves as analysts of financial statements rather than "watchers" of markets; as a result, they may miss important credit information embedded in market indexes such as stock prices and credit spreads. The diligent credit officer should make use of all available market indexes to monitor market perception of counterparty credit quality; these are powerful tools that can make monitoring a far more effective process — allowing time to reduce exposures before it is too late to take action. For instance, if a credit officer notices that Company ABC's stock price is falling and its bond credit spreads are widening, he may investigate the reasons for the moves. If, after examining these variables, he determines that the market is concerned about ABC's liquidity and access to short-term funding, he may opt to perform further due diligence by calling on the company to discuss its financial standing; alternatively, he may simply curtail further credit or instruct the trading desk to purchase credit protection on ABC. By simply waiting for the company to make a public statement about the performance of its stock and bonds and its possible liquidity problems, or by waiting until the release of the next financial statements, the credit officer might miss an opportunity to protect the firm's credit exposure. Monitoring information from the markets is thus an important part of the credit risk management process.

Summarizing the simple rules related to reporting and monitoring we note the following:

- If risks cannot be monitored they cannot be managed — if this occurs, a firm cannot be said to be in full control of its operations.
- Timeliness is important — reporting mechanisms that deliver 90% of a firm's risk picture efficiently can often be more effective than those that deliver 100% on a delayed basis; equally, mechanisms that are flexible, and can provide risk information in a multitude of formats to internal and external parties, are ideal.
- Generally speaking, more, rather than less, risk information and disclosure is beneficial — though it must be targeted at the correct audience and presented in a relevant fashion.
- Any effective reporting mechanism should be able to deliver an appropriate level of detail to the appropriate audience; senior managers should receive and review information that depicts the firm's risk without an excess of detail, while business, trading and risk managers should focus on information that is granular enough to run, or risk-manage, a business.
- Reporting on the source of profits and losses is a vital component of risk monitoring — if a firm is unable to explain its P&L it will not be able to understand, and therefore manage, its risks.
- Sensitivity to regulatory reporting requirements is also important to bear in mind — such reporting is important and will become more prominent over time; regulatory reports, however, are generally not sufficient to manage a business, meaning two reporting streams must be produced.
- Mechanisms to monitor top risks, collateral, counterparties, aged/illiquid inventories and other special risks should form part of the process as well; these can help identify potential risk problems before it is too late to take action.

7 Risk Management

Active management of risk is the core of trading/treasury, banking, business origination and independent risk control. Once a firm has established a governance process, identified and quantified its exposures and implemented monitoring and reporting mechanisms, it is ready to actively manage its risk. Ongoing management is the responsibility of trading and business unit managers, credit and market risk officers, and professionals from other control functions (including auditors, controllers, operations specialists and lawyers); each must play an active part in order to create an effective risk management culture. If business leaders introduce new risk management techniques but risk officers fail to keep pace, or controllers and auditors attempt to create a more secure environment but trading managers dismiss their efforts, a robust process will not emerge. Communication, prudence, experience and awareness are all central to the active management of exposure. While the management discipline makes use of a host of tools, models, analytics and reports, it is perhaps most reliant on the common sense and judgment of professionals charged with managing the risks; this is where the "art" of risk management moves to the forefront.

7.1 RISK MANAGERS SHOULD BE VISIBLE AND AVAILABLE

The independent risk management group is responsible for enforcing the firm's risk management directives on a daily basis. One of the most effective ways of accomplishing this task is to ensure credit and market risk officers are visible and available. Risk officers should work closely with traders, originators and business unit leaders, engage in regular communications and discussions with them, and be readily available to resolve risk management issues or queries. Active risk managers are typically consulted by business leaders for advice and counsel, while those that remain part of the "anonymous bureaucracy" of risk control are likely to be regarded as a hurdle that needs to be "overcome" in order to proceed with business — this does little to strengthen risk awareness. For example, a risk officer may make it part of her daily routine to spend time on trading floors, speak to trading managers and participate in morning origination and trading conference calls. Traders and originators will soon realize that the risk officer is available for discussion and consultation and is an effective link in the management and communication process. Market risk officers are often more "visible" than their control counterparts, as they spend more time in business and deal-related settings; however, it is just as important for credit, legal, financial and settlements specialists to be visible. Visibility and availability permit communication; communication strengthens risk management.

7.2 RISK OFFICERS AND RISK TAKERS SHOULD DISCUSS RISK ISSUES ON A REGULAR BASIS

Extending the rule above, it is useful for market and credit risk officers to communicate daily with trading managers, originators and other business leaders in order to consider risk matters of mutual interest and reinforce the governance process. Communication is often most effective when it is informal; a quick review of a handful of relevant risk issues can be very useful. In addition, communication should be "two-way" in nature in order to be constructive: business managers should receive, not only provide, information. Risk officers, aware of events and issues affecting the organization at large, can use daily meetings to provide information; the reciprocity generates goodwill and strengthens communications. If a market risk officer covering US corporate bond trading makes it a daily habit to review the top corporate bond risks, hedges and spread movements with the head of bond trading, he may also wish to provide an update on the firm's progress in other areas or discuss any significant risk, operational or systems issues/initiatives that are underway. This all forms part of the communication element that is so important in the daily management of risk.

7.3 RISK MANAGERS SHOULD BE IN REGULAR CONTACT WITH MARKET PARTICIPANTS — THE MARKET HAS A GREAT DEAL OF INFORMATION THAT CAN BE USED IN DAILY MANAGEMENT OF RISK

Since information is central to effective management of risks, it is essential for risk managers to be in continuous communication with traders, salespeople, bankers, research analysts and others with a view on markets, credits and events in the financial system; they should also have a regular dialog with external parties that are involved with particular markets or credits. Business leaders acting on the "front lines" are generally in an ideal position to learn about events that can directly impact exposures, and should be encouraged to share "breaking news" with risk officers. Having risk officers proximate to trading and banking floors can help in the process — being close to the source of information fosters stronger communication ties. For example, a trader, learning that a particular counterparty is having difficulty settling trades, can forward the information to the credit officer, who may wish to investigate the veracity of the information, the potential reasons for the settlement problems, and whether any protective action is warranted.

7.4 RISK MANAGERS SHOULD STRIVE TO BE "VALUE ADDED" BY SEARCHING FOR BENEFICIAL RISK SOLUTIONS WHENEVER POSSIBLE

The function of the risk process is to protect the firm and its shareholders from unexpected losses and other financial "surprises" by ensuring a sound operating environment. This means guiding a firm towards good, properly-priced risk opportunities. A process that rejects all risk may protect the firm from losses, but is unlikely to maximize shareholder value as the firm will be unable to generate revenues from its risk-related activities. Accordingly, a risk function that adds economic value while protecting the firm's resources might be regarded as benefiting the interests of the firm and the shareholder. Risk officers who have enough experience and knowledge to help a business unit transform a bad risk — one that generates too much risk for the profitability being offered — into a good risk can protect the firm while permitting profitable business to occur. For instance, a credit officer who rejects a proposed credit-sensitive transaction because it has "too much risk" is missing half of the risk/return equation; an officer who examines the same risk and attempts to restructure it by lowering the risk (to a level commensurate with the profitability being offered) helps transform bad risk into good risk and optimizes use of the firm's risk capital. Transforming the credit risk may involve the use of collateral, netting agreements, margining arrangements, credit default structures, and so on; while risk transformation may not always be possible, the diligent risk officer will make every attempt to do so. Similar types of transformations can, of course, be considered for market, liquidity and legal risks — risk managers should attempt to add value in the management of any risk the firm assumes.

7.5 RISK DECISIONS SHOULD BE DOCUMENTED CLEARLY IN ORDER TO AVOID ERRORS AND MISINTERPRETATION; GOOD DOCUMENTATION ESTABLISHES A PROPER AUDIT TRAIL

Clear documentation of all risk decisions is common sense and sound management. While maintaining good records may seem obvious, poor record-keeping is often a recurring problem; it may be attributable to lack of discipline, decisions taken higher up the management chain, exceptional decisions made by those in regional offices, and so forth. For instance, a senior risk manager, contacted for risk approval during "off hours" by a trader in another time zone, may simply fail to document the decision the following day. This can result in wasted hours trying to reconstruct what has, or has not, been approved, and by whom. A simple process of requiring every risk management decision to be properly documented and filed — whether in electronic or hardcopy form — helps eliminate misunderstandings and builds a strong audit trail; both are essential for risk control purposes and preservation of the firm's risk experience and "memory." There should be no exceptions to the documentation process.

7.6 WHEN A POTENTIAL RISK PROBLEM IS DISCOVERED, IMMEDIATE ACTION MUST BE TAKEN; PROBLEMS MUST NOT BE PERMITTED TO GROW OUT OF CONTROL

Many large risk-related problems begin as very small problems. They often grow and intensify because they are not managed early in the identification process, or because market events move quickly and cause losses to grow before action is taken. When any type of risk problem is encountered — credit, market, operational, legal, and so on — it is incumbent on the risk or control officer to take immediate action. This may involve solving the problem in conjunction with relevant business and control personnel, or elevating the issue to senior or executive managers. Regardless of the process, it is imperative to act on risk problems as soon as they are discovered. For instance, if a market risk officer responsible for coverage of yen interest rate derivatives notices, during the course of her review, that new trades are appearing under slightly different counterparty names — ABC Ltd., ABC Corp., ABC Intl. Corp. — she may feel that trade tickets are being entered erroneously, or that the firm is actually dealing with a variety of different counterparties under the ABC "umbrella." While not strictly a market risk issue, she determines that the matter should be investigated by operations and credit personnel, as it may be indicative of a broader problem — lack of discipline by sales/trading personnel in "knowing the client" or erroneous trades with counterparties in the ABC group that may not be sufficiently creditworthy.

7.7 RISK DECISIONS SHOULD NOT BE DRIVEN BY COMPETITIVE PRESSURES

When a competitor is thought to be engaged in a risk-related business, business managers may feel pressure to "follow the leader" by offering the same products or business lines. While there may be good reasons for considering a transaction or entering a business, doing so to follow another firm's lead is generally not sufficient. Risk managers encountering this argument must not assume that a competitor is actually engaging in a transaction or business without confirmation. In the "heat of the moment" misinformation can circulate between business managers and risk officers — it is therefore incumbent on the risk officer to verify all facts. Once the information has been verified, it still may not be advisable for the firm to enter the same business. Different firms are likely to have somewhat different risk philosophies, goals, expertise and profiles. While some may wish to enter many markets in order to satisfy client or proprietary requirements, others may wish to preserve a narrower focus in order to control costs and risks. Ultimately, the risk-bearing business undertaken by a firm must be consistent with its mandate, goals and risk appetite, and should not be driven by the actions (or supposed actions) of competitors. For instance, if a trader eager to win a large sterling bond underwriting indicates to the risk commitment committee that Bank XYZ is known to be bidding aggressively to win the same business, the committee may explore whether XYZ is actually bidding and, if so, whether the bid makes sense within a risk/return framework. The committee may find that XYZ is not bidding at all, that the bid is aggressive (perhaps too aggressive for the firm, given its own risk appetite and current exposure), or that the bid is commensurate with the risk being taken. No assumptions should be made on such matters — investigation, diligence and application of the firm's own standards are necessary operating procedures.

7.8 IF OTHER INSTITUTIONS DO NOT WANT TO ACCEPT A RISK-BEARING DEAL, THERE MAY BE A REASON FOR IT — IT IS IMPORTANT TO DETERMINE WHETHER IT SHOULD BE A FACTOR IN APPROVING OR DECLINING THE RISK

Extending the rule above, it is easy to consider a reverse scenario: if market knowledge suggests that more than one institution has declined to execute a risk-bearing transaction, it is good practice to investigate the underlying reasons; though such information may be difficult to obtain, it is worth the effort. The investigation may reveal that the underlying credit and market risks are too large, the exposures are illiquid and unhedgeable, or that some other factors are at work to create more risk than expected or desired; alternatively, economic returns may not be commensurate with potential risks. While these factors should ideally be brought to light during the identification and quantification stages, preliminary investigation by risk takers can save time and effort. For instance, if a market risk officer is asked to review a potential long-dated derivative trade and learns that several other firms have opted not to bid on the structure, he may undertake a more thorough analysis to determine the presence of any "hidden" risks. The risk officer may learn that the proposed transaction has an odd cash flow structure and reference index that will render it difficult to hedge without the assumption of significant basis risk; he may then decline the trade, determine whether it can be restructured into a more manageable form, or investigate if sufficient risk premium can be obtained to cover the perceived risks.

7.9 PRUDENT RISK RESERVE MECHANISMS SHOULD BE ESTABLISHED FOR CONCENTRATED, COMPLEX, ILLIQUID OR MARKED-TO-MODEL RISKS

An effective reserve mechanism, part of any prudent risk management process, allows for the creation of a financial buffer to protect against the uncertainties of risk, models, illiquid markets, and so forth. An appropriate mechanism permits reserves to be taken and released objectively rather than subjectively; the objective process is automatic, transparent and straightforward, and does not allow subjective views or opinions to influence the process. For instance, if a firm's derivative desk assumes a long-term volatility risk, a set percentage of the risk or anticipated P&L may be set aside automatically; when the risk is fully neutralized or the deal is unwound, the reserve can be released back into P&L. Under a subjective approach risk officers and business managers might jointly review the risks of a transaction (or portfolio or business line) and determine appropriate reserves on a case-by-case basis; the release of reserves might also be done in joint consultation. While this type of mechanism is better than having none at all, it may leave too much to interpretation.

Different risks can draw different reserving levels. Special attention should be given to exposures that risk officers and business managers are especially concerned about, including those that are large, illiquid, long-dated, esoteric or model-centric. Such risks typically carry a higher probability or magnitude of loss, and must therefore be adequately reserved. Regardless of the reserving mechanism selected, risk officers should work with their finance colleagues in creating and applying a disciplined process. The board and risk committee should sanction methodologies that are developed, and should receive regular communication on the status of risks and reserves.

7.10 CREDIT RESERVE MECHANISMS SHOULD BE IMPLEMENTED IN ORDER TO ENCOURAGE ACTIVE MANAGEMENT OF CREDIT RISKS

An extension of the rule above relates to the creation of credit risk reserves. While it has become quite customary for firms to establish reserves against different market risks, it is still relatively rare, outside the commercial banking sector, for institutions to create dynamic credit reserves on credit-sensitive transactions with all counterparties. Even within the commercial banking world, the focus has historically been on reserves for impaired credits, with no allowances taken for creditworthy entities. Since certain firms that account for positions on a daily mark-to-market basis have a desire to actively manage credit exposures, the creation of a credit risk reserve mechanism emerges as a logical element of the process. By assigning a credit risk reserve to every transaction with every counterparty (based on dynamically changing exposure amounts and probabilities of default), a firm is able to price in the cost of credit. Once a cost of credit is obtained for multiple deals with a given client, it becomes relatively straightforward to allocate risk capital in support of credit-sensitive businesses, make optimal risk/return decisions and utilize credit derivative instruments to actively manage, and reshape, the firm's credit risk profile. These are powerful tools that permit dynamic management of credit risk.

7.11 FAILURE TO PRICE THE COST OF CREDIT RISK WILL ULTIMATELY LEAD TO A MISBALANCED CREDIT PORTFOLIO AND CREDIT LOSSES

In Chapter 2 we noted the importance of properly pricing risk. While this is common practice when dealing with market and liquidity risks, it is only beginning to gain momentum in the field of credit risk, which has not traditionally been the focus of pricing discussion. Failure by a firm to appropriately price credit risk will result in a misbalancing of its credit portfolio, leading to an excess of credit losses. For instance, if a firm does not routinely price its credit risk exposure, it is likely to show the most competitive bid in the market (compared to institutions that take full account of credit pricing). This means it will win an overly large share of business, including business that will fail to perform as expected. As a result of this misbalancing, credit losses will exceed an anticipated average, and will tend towards unexpected, or extreme, levels; this will eventually exhaust any credit reserves that have been established and will begin eroding capital. Properly pricing credit risk will cause the firm to alternately win and lose business, depending on the nature of the counterparty and transaction, the construction of the portfolio and the state of the markets. In the medium-term its risk profile will be more appropriately balanced and the extension of credit will be profitable.

7.12 A RISK IS NOT HEDGED OR SOLD UNTIL IT IS ACTUALLY HEDGED OR SOLD; JUST BECAUSE IT IS "THEORETICALLY" POSSIBLE TO HEDGE OR SELL A RISK DOES NOT MEAN THAT IT CAN BE DONE

While most risk managers derive comfort from the fact that a deal or transaction can be hedged or sold in order to reduce or eliminate risk, it is important to remember that risk is retained until the actual hedge or sale is consummated. It is not uncommon for trading managers to discuss the theoretical hedging options associated with a deal, or for sales managers to refer to clients who are interested in purchasing a given position or risk. Traders and salespeople are required to think in such terms and can add value to the risk management process by illuminating possible risk mitigants. However, such mitigants only have value once they are completed. Until that time, theoretical "exit strategies" must be regarded as theoretical. Hedges and sales can disappear quickly if market conditions change or deal pricing does not materialize as expected. For instance, a risk commitment committee reviewing a potential fixed price underwriting for an emerging markets issuer may take comfort in the fact that the sales team believes the deal will be oversubscribed if launched at a particular price. However, until the deal is priced and the client orders are confirmed, the commitment committee must view the underwriting as a full risk to the firm. Any risk decision by the committee must, therefore, be undertaken in accordance with risk limits and other directives set forth through the governance process.

7.13 ACTIVE MANAGEMENT OF ASSET AND FUNDING LIQUIDITY IS VITAL IN ORDER TO AVOID POTENTIAL LOSSES

As indicated in previous chapters liquidity — the ability to realize or fund a position — is central to the prudent financial management of a firm; the onset of illiquidity has the potential to create significant losses by destroying value, and can sometimes do so very quickly. A firm must be aware of both asset and funding liquidity. Asset liquidity relates to the ability to sell or transfer a position — on-balance sheet, such as a bond, loan or stock — or off-balance sheet, such as a derivative. Funding, or liability, liquidity relates to the ability to obtain and use funding to meet financial obligations, collateral calls, margin payments, losses, and so on. A firm may not encounter any liquidity problems if it is not forced to liquidate assets or arrange funding in a crisis setting. However, it is very difficult to know when, or if, a liquidity crisis will strike; accordingly, precautionary measures must always be considered. In trading, financial or market-driven businesses, where a considerable amount of a firm's success is based on the availability of liquidity, preserving confidence in business operations is absolutely essential. While firms that manufacture capital goods can generally cope with temporary loss of confidence, the same is not true for a firm that relies on confidence and reputation to conduct business. Loss of either can lead to a liquidity squeeze; in the extreme, a squeeze can lead to outright failure. Being able to cope with liquidity contingencies is therefore vital. Many risk crises have arisen as a result of illiquidity. For instance, the collapse of Askin Management in 1994, a fund which was heavily invested in esoteric, and highly illiquid, mortgage backed securities and derivatives, occurred because institutions providing the fund with repurchase agreement financing were unwilling to repurchase the instruments at Askin's market prices as interest rates rose; had the fund possessed a greater amount of liquid securities with transparent market prices and two-way activity, the liquidity-induced collapse might have been averted.

When an institution's balance sheet is comprised of illiquid assets — generally large, risky or esoteric positions — it runs the danger of being unable to unwind risks and/or finance its operations. For instance, large positions are often illiquid under the best of market circumstances, and can be completely illiquid during times of market stress. If a firm has a very large position in a high yield bond marked at what it believes are conservative levels, and funds the position on a repo (repurchase agreement) basis, it may feel that it is managing its operations properly. However, if a market crisis unfolds, the price of the high yield bond drops and the repo finance provider calls for more collateral or terminates the financing, the firm faces considerable liquidity risk — it may try to sell the bond at a discount and repay the financing, put up collateral in another form or fund the position through alternate sources if the bond cannot be sold; any of these may result in incremental economic costs or outright losses. Carefully controlling and managing any position that is illiquid, or has the potential of becoming illiquid, is central to prudent risk management. Risk officers and trading managers must watch for signs that markets, market sectors, instruments or risks are becoming illiquid; as warning signs appear, preventive measures should be taken. While proactive management of illiquid risks related to market factors (e.g. interest rates, currencies, equities, and so on) is generally the focus of control, the same can apply to credit risks. Though many credit risks are, by definition, illiquid (e.g. non-tradable contracts between two parties), mechanisms can protect against further loss of value in an illiquid credit (e.g. shorting a corporate obligation, purchasing a spread or default option, and so on). It is worth stressing that the damaging effects of illiquidity are not limited to large positions; esoteric or complex risk positions, and even small positions which have fallen out of favor, can be impacted by the same forces.

Funding liquidity risk must also be managed actively. If a firm lacks a robust funding program it may find itself in financial difficulties in the event of market problems. Once a firm's funding sources are known to be in jeopardy, further short-term credit may be suspended, compounding the problem and generating a liquidity spiral; this may ultimately lead to losses and outright default. Funding must at all times be as certain as possible, and should typically be drawn from multiple sources and cover various maturities. If one market cannot be accessed at a particular time, a firm should be able to turn to alternate markets. In addition, a firm should seek committed funding sources whenever possible, so they cannot be withdrawn in the event of rapid deterioration; this ensures continued access to financing in bad market conditions, or when lenders might otherwise wish to curtail funding.

A well-designed liquidity management program, often constructed by the independent risk management and treasury functions, ensures that assets and liabilities remain as liquid and stable as possible. Since liquidity is so important, mechanisms that constrain and track possible sources of illiquidity emerge as important management tools. As noted in Chapter 6, control units may wish to prepare aged and illiquid position reports so business and risk management can focus on problem areas. From a liability perspective, a firm should arrange a broad range of well-diversified, and committed, funding alternatives, and monitor the market's perception of the firm's credit/funding access on a regular basis.

Active management of liquidity risk is so important that it forms one of the "cardinal rules."

7.14 SINCE LIQUIDITY HAS A TENDENCY TO DISAPPEAR QUICKLY, CONSERVATIVE LIQUIDATION ASSUMPTIONS SHOULD BE USED WHEN MANAGING RISKS

A corollary to the liquidity rule above relates to the use of conservative liquidation periods when making risk management decisions. Liquidation often takes longer than anticipated, and may occur during a period of market stress. Since a firm must assume that liquidity will disappear very rapidly, conservative liquidation periods that span days, weeks or months should be applied to risk exposures (including proprietary risk positions and collateral taken to secure credit exposures). In addition to the market dynamics of specific asset classes (e.g. it is easier to liquidate a position in US Treasuries than in emerging market bonds), a firm must take account of the size of its position and any other factors that might influence its ability to sell or cover. Obviously, the larger or more complex a position, the longer the liquidation period, and the greater the potential erosion in value. Risk officers must also consider the fact that positions and collateral tend to be liquidated during times of market stress — precisely when internal pressure to reduce risk mounts, others are exiting the market or counterparties to trades default; an additional allowance must be made for the extra time it might take to unwind a risk. For example, if a firm knows from experience that it normally takes 24 hours to cover a large position in the 20-year sterling swap market it may scale its VAR or risk limits according to such a benchmark; however, this timescale may underestimate the true risk of the position in poor market conditions. For instance, the firm may have learned during a previous crisis that 20-year swap liquidity disappeared quickly, lengthening the hedge coverage time from one to five business days. The 20-year swap position may thus carry five times more risk than the firm believes; accordingly, when setting and managing risk limits it may wish to scale its risk by a factor that reflects possible illiquidity. While the scaling factor need not be based on a disaster scenario, some prudent middle ground might be appropriate.

7.15 AN INVESTMENT ACCOUNT MUST NOT BE REGARDED AS A TRADING ACCOUNT FOR ILLIQUID POSITIONS

An investment account, which is distinct from a marked-to-market trading account, is designed to accommodate long-term investments. Rather than revaluing investment assets on a daily basis — as is customary through mark-to-market conventions — an investment account allows for periodic valuation at the lower of cost or market prices; changes are reflected through the equity account of the balance sheet rather than the income statement. Since the accounting regulations governing assets that can be moved from trading into investment accounts are reasonably well established, there is typically very little concern about the nature of the assets that can be included, the length of time they must "reside" in the account, when and how they may be sold or transferred, and so on. However, control officers should still scrutinize investment account activity. Under no circumstances should an account be used to warehouse illiquid or unsaleable assets; the account should not become a "dumping ground" for assets that a firm no longer favors and which it is unable to sell — and for which it no longer wants to reflect daily P&L movement. For instance, if a trading desk has a large portfolio of high yield bonds that it wants to place in an investment account solely because it does not want to show daily P&L fluctuations, it should not be permitted to do so by those in the control structure; such a scheme is only intended to attract different accounting treatment and move the bonds off the "front line" of monitoring and scrutiny.

7.16 LARGE DEALS MEAN LARGE — AND POSSIBLY ILLIQUID OR UNHEDGEABLE — RISKS; THEY MUST BE MANAGED CAREFULLY AND COMMAND AN APPROPRIATE PREMIUM

Relating two concepts discussed in previous chapters — liquidity and risk compensation — it is worth noting that when a firm is engaged in large transactions with significant credit or market risks, it must manage the positions with care and ensure the risk premium levied is sufficient to cover risks that may be unhedgeable (and are almost certainly illiquid). Mispricing large risks may ultimately create losses within a firm's trading or credit portfolio. For example, if a firm is bidding on a large equity block trade — equal, perhaps, to two or three weeks of trading volume — it must ensure that its bid reflects the risks generated by a position that is effectively illiquid. Since the firm will be forced to sell any residual position on a gradual basis, into a hostile market, it may sustain significant losses; accordingly, its risk pricing must reflect the premium and the position must be managed with extreme care in order to minimize the possibility of problems. The same discipline should, of course, apply to all other large risk exposures.

7.17 CONCENTRATED RISKS CAN BE VERY DAMAGING AND MUST BE MANAGED ACTIVELY

Concentrated positions — in securities, derivatives, credit exposures, and so forth — can be very damaging. Most firms realize that diversification is essential to prudent risk management and do their best to avoid situations where they are not properly diversified; this helps minimize the likelihood of losses. When a concentration is unavoidable — where business imperatives require assumption of a concentrated risk, or a mispriced deal leaves a large residual, for example — it must be monitored carefully; where possible the concentration should be protected through a proxy hedge or a defensive reserve. Care must also be taken to price the position properly. In order to identify and track concentrations within a large risk-taking firm, systems and reporting infrastructure must be of sufficient depth and breadth to identify and flag all concentrated exposures. While a single desk with a particular risk might not believe it is concentrated, an aggregate view of a firm's entire risk operation may indicate otherwise. For instance, if a firm trades corporate bonds in the primary global bond markets (e.g. the US domestic market, the Euromarket, the Samurai market, and so on), individual traders may build positions in the bonds of a given corporate issuer. When positions from four or five markets are consolidated, the firm may find it has a large concentration in the credit spread and default risk of that issuer, and may be forced to sell down or purchase default protection in order to remain within the firm's aggregate limits. Being able to monitor cross-product and regional positions is essential to managing concentrations.

7.18 RISK TAKERS SHOULD BE LIMITED TO TAKING RISK IN SPECIFIC MARKETS AND INSTRUMENTS

One of the most effective ways of ensuring an efficient and well-controlled trading environment is to limit risk takers to specific risk activities. Under this structure, risk takers are restricted to products, instruments and deals that are central to their core markets and expertise. By instilling this discipline a firm ensures that the true "experts" in a particular risk category are the only ones that are actually taking and managing the risk. Such an approach creates wiser risk-taking and results in a more efficient use of capital. For instance, a trader responsible for making markets in European equities should not be permitted to "day trade" or position risk outside the core European equity market. While there may be a need to consider macro hedges in other global equity markets and, possibly, select currencies (in order to hedge foreign client orders, and so on), the trader should only position risk in European equities. If a firm feels it is missing opportunities by not having cross-market trading capabilities, it might consider the establishment of a separate risk-taking unit that is permitted to take risk across various products, asset classes and markets; such a unit might be given broad authority to trade independently of the actions of "traditional" experts (who remain focused on, and committed to, their own strategies). By enforcing a strict product discipline a firm is also able to control its risk profile more efficiently and ensure that risk capital is being employed optimally — it eliminates the chance that offsetting risks are taken or that risks are doubled up, and forces risk takers to remain focused on their areas of expertise.

7.19 RISK-BEARING POSITIONS MUST BE BOOKED/HOUSED IN OFFICIALLY SANCTIONED TRADING SYSTEMS

Risks cannot be identified, monitored or controlled if they do not reside in an authorized trading system; a firm that permits its risk takers to position risks without having them flow through an officially sanctioned trading platform is unlikely to be in control of its business or exposures. It is not sufficient for trade tickets to be entered into isolated electronic spreadsheets or databases that have no connection to the firm's books and records or financial processing modules; this is equivalent to having them written on paper. Rather, an appropriate trading mechanism, with strong links to middle and back-office functionality, must be employed. Any position that generates risk must be included in such mechanisms, without exception. As part of the process, financial controllers need to reconcile trade blotters, tickets and confirmations against records contained in systems — by doing so, a firm can avoid operational errors and fraud (e.g. "ticket in the drawer" problems) and can ensure proper monitoring capabilities. On a related note, risk takers should not be permitted to trade through off-premises systems; such platforms are generally not robust or properly linked with settlements processes and may be subject to manipulation.

7.20 USING FINANCIAL INCENTIVES AND PENALTIES TO INFLUENCE RISK-TAKING BEHAVIOR IS AN EFFECTIVE MANAGEMENT TOOL

In order to direct risk-taking behavior and influence the shape of a firm's risk profile, management should use all available tools. As indicated in Chapter 3, explicit enforcement and governance tools, such as new product processes, commitment committees, policies and risk limits, are a fundamental dimension of the process. However, other mechanisms can also be considered, including those that have a direct financial impact on the desk or manager responsible for a given risk. Imposing penalties to alter the shape of the risk profile or introduce a greater amount of liquidity is one such mechanism. For instance, a firm may wish to minimize the amount of aged or illiquid inventory it holds. While such risk positions may be housed under existing risk limits (and thus not be in violation of any corporate policy), they may ultimately cause problems when financial markets start to weaken — risk positions that are illiquid in good market cycles are likely to become even more illiquid during market downturns, necessitating larger markdowns. Accordingly, management may want its business leaders to review and reduce their illiquid risks on a continuous basis. In order to do so the firm may impose financial charges on the business unit's P&L, equal to a set percentage of the market value, that scale up the longer the positions remain on the books. Failure to liquidate aged positions will result in a loss on two fronts: continual markdowns as controllers insist on lower prices in the absence of sales, and aging penalties that are applied to any position on the books in excess of 60 (or 90 or 180) days. Since traders and business managers are likely to be compensated based on their financial performance, they will attempt to avoid any penalties that detract from such performance — including those applied to illiquid inventory. Similar penalties can be applied to other areas that present potential concerns or challenges. Financial incentives can also be used to influence behavior and risk-taking activity. For example, a firm may credit a trading area's P&L when it sources a client for an illiquid risk on another desk's book; this can help focus attention on "problem risks" among a broader group of financial professionals, some of whom may have different contacts or accounts interested in assuming a particular risk. By providing a financial incentive to those in the firm who can help reduce other pockets of problem risk, the entire firm benefits.

7.21 AGGRESSIVE RISK-TAKING BEHAVIOR, WHICH MAY ULTIMATELY CREATE RISK PROBLEMS, SHOULD BE MANAGED CLOSELY

Firms that permit aggressive risk-taking on a regular basis may eventually be forced to deal with large losses. Aggressive risk-taking, within approved risk limits, can manifest itself in many different forms. For instance, trading managers may be tempted to generate what they view as "risk-free" (or nearly "risk-free") income by selling deeply out-of-the-money options that have a very remote chance of ending with value; the most aggressive managers may leave positions completely unhedged in order to enhance upfront profitability. No credit exposure is incurred on such trades and traditional market risk measures might not register much sensitivity (e.g. negative gamma). However, any sharp market move can propel such options closer-to-the-money, generating large losses. Accordingly, prudent risk management calls for discipline in limiting the sale of unhedged, out-of-the-money options. The same type of philosophy must apply in aggressive bidding for large block trades or "bought deals." While a firm may find it tempting to bid very aggressively to win such "marquis" business, an inability to very quickly sell the block through an institutional client base can result in very large losses. This is particularly true since the business environment is very competitive — once the winner has the block on its books the market quickly becomes aware of the position and is likely to want to disrupt smooth placement. Strict limits and sensible pricing parameters are essential in order to minimize or avoid losses. Other "aggressive" risk behavior should be monitored closely.

7.22 RISK MITIGATION SHOULD NOT BE MISTAKEN FOR RISK MIGRATION

It is common, in the financial world, to substitute one type of risk for another. This is an acceptable practice and, if executed properly, can prove to be a profitable affair. However, a transaction that is put on to hedge, reduce or otherwise mitigate a risk is generally not a riskless trade. Rather, a firm is likely to be substituting one risk for another — effectively transforming a "risk mitigation" device into a "risk migration" device. For instance, if an industrial manufacturer uses copper in its manufacturing process, it has a natural input exposure to copper prices. It is concerned that rising copper prices will reduce profit margins, and can mitigate the exposure by purchasing a copper derivative. When the price of copper rises, the company pays more for its copper, but receives a financial gain from the derivative — it has thus mitigated its copper price risk. In reality, however, it has actually converted the copper price risk into a credit risk; the risk has been transformed, or migrated, from one form to another. If the company is creating a copper hedge through a listed exchange, it may regard that credit exposure as non-existent; if it is relying on the performance of a counterparty through the OTC market, it has a more significant credit exposure. Thus, the company no longer has risk exposure to copper prices — as long as the OTC counterparty continues to perform. If the counterparty fails and copper prices have risen, the firm will have to replace the hedge transaction in the marketplace at a loss. Migration can, of course, assume many other forms. For instance, if a bank wants to reduce its credit exposure to a particular counterparty, it can short the company's bond or purchase a credit derivative on the company's credit performance. While it may mitigate the original credit exposure, as intended, it has migrated its risk to interest rates (if shorting a bond) or another counterparty's credit (if entering into a derivative).

7.23 RISK MITIGATION/MIGRATION TOOLS SHOULD BE USED WHEREVER POSSIBLE

Continuing with the theme above, firms have access to a broad range of tools and instruments to mitigate or migrate credit, market, legal and operational risks. These should be considered and used whenever appropriate as a mechanism for actively managing the firm's risk profile. While risk-taking firms assume risks in order to earn a return, there are times when it makes greater sense to reduce, transfer or otherwise alter exposures. For instance, if a bank wants to enter into a credit-sensitive financial relationship with a sub-investment grade counterparty (expecting to capitalize, perhaps, on other dimensions of business), but the credit officer feels uncomfortable extending credit, alternate risk mitigating/migrating solutions should be sought. The counterparty might be willing to post upfront collateral to secure trades or enter into a mark-to-market agreement where it collateralizes the market value of any exposure that builds to a positive level. Alternatively, the firm might purchase a credit default swap from a creditworthy firm to cover any exposure generated by the sub-investment grade counterparty (with an appropriate charge back to the counterparty for the risk premium paid on the default swap in order not to misbalance credit risks). These arrangements might give the firm enough comfort to proceed with credit-sensitive business. Other types of mitigation and migration techniques can be applied to defease the effects of various classes of risk. For instance, if a firm is asked to bid on a bond deal for a corporate issuer, but is uncertain about the exact market clearing level, it may choose to bid on a "best efforts" basis by selling as many bonds as possible at the clearing price — but not committing to sell the entire block at a fixed price. Or, if the firm has to bid "firm," it may choose to mitigate the "disaster" risk by incorporating a "material adverse change" clause, allowing it to withdraw its commitment if a significant issuer or market event disrupts its ability to price and place the bonds. Alternatively, it may purchase a spreadlock, guaranteeing it a fixed spread in relation to a fluctuating benchmark. Business and risk managers should make use of these, and other, risk mitigation/migration techniques whenever possible.

7.24 ATTEMPTING TO PREDICT WHAT WILL HAPPEN IN THE FUTURE IS HAZARDOUS — THE RISK FUNCTION SHOULD BE REALISTIC IN ASSESSING THE TIME HORIZON OF DEALS, STRUCTURES AND CREDITS

Business and risk managers often attempt to predict the future outcome of market moves, counterparty performance, and so on. While that is certainly part of their job — they must, after all, make some estimate of what might happen to the deals and risks being assumed — it should be kept to the realm of the plausible and useful. For instance, credit officers might be called on to assess the creditworthiness and financial viability of a counterparty over periods spanning 10, or more, years; this is an obvious requirement when a firm is considering extending long-term, unsecured credit through a loan or derivative. Predicting the likely financial performance of a company over an extended period of time is a difficult — and arguably impossible — task; expecting a credit officer to have complete confidence in his or her assessment of long-term creditworthiness is somewhat fanciful. For instance, if a credit officer determines a credit is of A-rated quality (solid investment grade) it may approve a 10-year unsecured swap transaction on that basis; in the absence of any documentary protection to the contrary (such as the right to obtain collateral in the event the counterparty is downgraded to sub-investment grade status), the firm is left with little protective recourse should the credit deteriorate to a precarious sub-investment grade level in seven years; with three years left until the trade concludes, the firm still faces considerable probability of loss and may be forced to purchase a default swap in order to protect itself. The difficulty in projecting the future creditworthiness of a counterparty is obviously a significant challenge. In the same light, a risk manager or trader might have difficulty opining on the liquidity of a hedge instrument five or 10 years in the future. Credits and markets change with frequency, and there are no guarantees that assumptions related to creditworthiness, liquidity, hedgeability, and so on will hold true five, seven, or 10 years hence. When this problem presents itself it is best to be realistic about what can and cannot be predicted; since decisions still have to be made, a conservative judgment is often best. This may mean pricing in a greater risk premium (to compensate for the unknown) or establishing long-term risk reserves that can be used to cover potential losses generated by changing markets and conditions. Above all, the risk function should always remain realistic in its abilities to predict the course of future events.

7.25 UNDERSTANDING WHY A CLIENT IS ENTERING INTO A COMPLEX RISK TRADE IS IMPORTANT; IF SUITABILITY EMERGES AS AN ISSUE, IT SHOULD BE MADE KNOWN TO LEGAL OFFICERS

Over the years, client suitability has emerged as an important, and often contentious, risk and business management issue. Even before being brought to the forefront by cases such as Procter and Gamble, Gibson Greetings, Orange County, and others, the issue generated debate on the correct approach toward offering complex risk and investment products. Certain financial products are characterized by structural complexities or large amounts of leverage; these can create significant losses or gains, or provide/remove risk protection at particular points in time. For many sophisticated clients, with appropriate expertise and management authorization, such products are perfectly appropriate — regardless of their inherent riskiness. For less sophisticated clients the same may not be true. Such clients may not always understand the level of risk they are assuming or how their risk and payoff profiles change with market events. Accordingly, when risk officers find that a complex or highly leveraged trade is being contemplated with an end-user, it is prudent to bring the matter to the attention of legal officers and sales/relationship business managers. They can opine on the structure of the transaction and the nature of the client's legal capacity to know and understand the deal being contemplated. Indeed, some firms institutionalize the process by making client suitability review part of the governance process. They may also create minimum disclosure standards related to upfront and ongoing risk exposure, maximum downside scenarios in the event of a market crisis, and so on. Whenever there is any doubt about the capacity of a client to understand, or its ability to legally enter into, a deal, a firm may wish to restructure or decline the transaction.

7.26 STRONG CLIENT SALES PRACTICES CAN HELP MITIGATE RISKS

As previous experiences have shown, a firm that is focused on providing its clients with the strongest possible sales practices and support benefits on two fronts — it builds a deeper relationship with its clients and reduces the possibility that it will encounter risk management problems in the future. The cases of Procter and Gamble and Gibson Greetings (among others) have demonstrated the importance of conducting client relationships in a positive manner and adhering to the fiduciary/advisor relationship; indeed, in the aftermath of the derivatives debacles of 1994–1995, voluntary "codes of conduct" — which codified new sales practices — became more prevalent among derivative providers active in the marketplace. Implementing a strong sales practice means treating customers fairly (e.g. not trying to take advantage of their inexperience or lack of knowledge in order to generate economic profit), acting with care and diligence in developing client risk strategies, ensuring that client needs are well understood and strategies being marketed are designed to address their needs, and making sure that an appropriate level of disclosure accompanies all financial dealings. These basic concepts generate goodwill and lead to business; they are also likely to minimize misunderstandings and, in more extreme circumstances, challenges or lawsuits. Adhering to such sales practices enables a firm to mitigate its own risks by ensuring transactions will not be reversed and exposures will not have to be replaced or rehedged.

7.27 EXECUTING A RISK-BEARING DEAL TO ACCOMMODATE A CLIENT OR BUILD A CLIENT RELATIONSHIP DOES NOT JUSTIFY THE ASSUMPTION OF BAD RISK

We have noted that assuming risk without being properly compensated is likely to lead to a misbalancing of the portfolio and may ultimately lead to an excess of credit or market risk losses. Extending this logic, it is generally not advisable to use risk-bearing transactions to win or build a client relationship if that risk is bad — that is, if the risk is not priced properly or negatively impacts the risk portfolio. Though some firms use risk-based products as a mechanism for gaining client business (e.g. using balance sheet and credit facilities to win lucrative underwriting and advisory assignments), this strategy is only sustainable when the risks being offered are "smart" for the firm — that is, when the risks are priced appropriately and fit within the business unit's overall mandate and directives. In the short-run assuming a "bad risk" may be written off as the cost of gaining new business or deepening a client relationship (e.g. a "loss leader"); in the medium and long-term this type of strategy is ill-advised. For instance, if a firm attempting to build an important client account enters into a multi-year derivative deal that generates no profit (e.g. market and credit risks have not been factored into the pricing), the firm has a long-term risk that will consume capital and require active management — but earn no profit. If a market or credit event moves against the position, there is nothing to protect the firm, and it will have sustained losses on two fronts — lack of upfront return and losses from back-end market/credit risks.

7.28 WHERE POSSIBLE AND FEASIBLE — AND WITHOUT COMPROMISING CONFIDENTIALITY — COUNTERPARTY INFORMATION SHOULD BE SHARED WITH OTHERS SEEKING TO EXTEND CREDIT

Financial crises often demonstrate the need for firms to share a certain amount of information on the creditworthiness of counterparties that are known to take substantial risk. While care must be taken not to share sensitive, non-public information, breach competitive rules, or advise business units of information coming from credit functions of other firms, considerable benefits can be gained by sharing information between credit functions. This process can help ensure that all parties understand the relative magnitude of the risks being considered (or undertaken) by the target counterparty and may help protect against the extension of imprudent amounts of credit that could impact the system at large. Again, due care must be taken not to breach any legal, "Chinese Wall" or anti-competitive issues. If this can be safely arranged, the end result is likely to be a more informed credit sector and a more secure financial system. For instance, if a credit officer at a bank notices that various requests for leverage have been submitted for a particular hedge fund, she may wish to consult with credit counterparts at other firms in order to determine whether a cautionary note should be sounded; again, communication must occur within the boundaries defined by legal officers.

7.29 COLLATERAL TAKEN IN SUPPORT OF AN EXPOSURE SHOULD RELATE DIRECTLY TO COUNTERPARTY CREDIT QUALITY, THE SIZE OF THE RISK EXPOSURE AND RELEVANT CONCENTRATION/LIQUIDITY PARAMETERS

Effective management of risks means that collateralized credit exposures must be appropriately secured — under any market scenario. Though different firms have different thresholds after which they require collateral, a fundamental rule applicable to all firms is that collateral taken in support of a transaction must relate directly to the quality of the counterparty, the size of the risk exposure and any concentration and liquidity parameters that might influence the exposure. Thus, a very high quality credit typically requires no collateral (unless existing exposures grow very large), while a borderline investment grade credit might require collateral for long-dated deals; sub-investment grade credits might require collateral on every deal. Large exposures on volatile underlying indexes (which have the potential to generate more credit exposure over the life of the transaction, or until the next valuation and collateral call period) must be secured by a greater amount of collateral in order to provide an adequate cushion. Equally, transactions that are based on very concentrated or illiquid risks (either the underlying deal itself or the collateral taken in support of a deal) should carry a greater amount of protection. In the event of counterparty default, a firm may find itself unable to liquidate collateral quickly enough to cover its exposure — leaving it unsecured. Thus, if a firm has entered into derivative transactions with a counterparty and secures the replacement value with corporate bond collateral, it may be left with an unsecured exposure if the value of the collateral deteriorates more rapidly than expected; if the counterparty defaults, the firm will become an unsecured bankruptcy creditor.

7.30 LEGAL AND OPERATIONAL STAFF SHOULD BE FAMILIAR WITH TRIGGERS AND CLAUSES THAT CAN BE INFLUENCED BY CREDIT, MARKET AND LIQUIDITY EVENTS

Various aspects of risk management are governed by legal and operational issues that must be implemented properly and followed diligently. For instance, derivative transactions written under ISDA agreements, as well as credits granted under loan agreements, often contain rating downgrade triggers and financial covenants that provide the credit provider with additional protection allowing for unwind, prepayment or collateral draws. Likewise, credit-sensitive transactions might be supported by collateral that must be continuously revalued in order to obtain additional cover as market prices deteriorate or exposures increase. Legal and operational staff should be sufficiently familiar with the essential components of legal triggers, clauses and covenants to know when to take actions that can protect the firm's risk profile. The same applies to operations and settlement staff responsible for monitoring collateral values and other transaction settlement details. Having control officers act as a first, and important, line of defense in collateral/trigger issues strengthens the overall risk management process; any actions that need to be taken should be done in consultation with relevant risk personnel. For example, a collateral specialist following the collateral portfolio of a "watchlist" counterparty and noticing that security coverage has dropped rapidly from one day to the next as a result of a spike in exposure may place a call for additional collateral and immediately contact the credit officer to relay the findings; the credit officer may elect to curtail any new dealings until the incremental collateral is received.

7.31 LEGAL DOCUMENTATION THAT PROTECTS MULTIPLE PRODUCTS/EVENTUALITIES CAN HELP CONTROL RISK EXPOSURES

Legal professionals play an important role in the risk management process by ensuring appropriate legal documentation is used to control exposures. Wherever possible, it is advisable to use the most flexible documentary templates available. For instance, derivative documentation that covers cross-product obligations and allows for the broadest level of netting and set-off rights can be advantageous when counterparty default occurs. Instead of having each individual trade in a derivative or financing portfolio evaluated by a bankruptcy judge, an entire portfolio of products is condensed into a single payable or receivable (eliminating the risk of "cherry picking"). Accordingly, multi-product, multi-currency master agreements can be a very useful risk management tool, and efforts directed at implementing such agreements are well worthwhile. Likewise, loan agreements with financial covenants (e.g. minimum ownership, maximum leverage levels) that require the repayment of a loan/posting of security upon breach can help protect a firm. Full advantage should be taken of these documentation structures to help mitigate risk exposures.

7.32 A LEGAL DOCUMENTATION BACKLOG MAY ULTIMATELY LEAD TO OPERATIONAL/LEGAL ERRORS AND LOSSES — AUTHORIZATIONS, GUARANTEES, CONFIRMATIONS AND MASTER AGREEMENTS SHOULD ALWAYS BE AS CURRENT AS POSSIBLE

We have mentioned the importance of legal documentation in the creation of an effective risk management framework. The breadth of documentation is large and can include trade confirmations, ISDA or repurchase master netting agreements, collateral and margining agreements, bank loan and syndication documents, and so on. Allowing a documentation backlog to develop can create significant operational and legal risks by denying a firm the protections afforded by such documentation; indeed, failure to arrange appropriate documentation exposes a firm to as much risk as any other failure in the risk management process. A documentation backlog is created whenever a trade, transaction or deal is arranged, as relevant legal documents generally cannot be produced instantaneously. In some cases the backlog can be resolved very quickly — trade confirmations, for instance, can be generated automatically and distributed within minutes or hours of a deal; they then need to be confirmed and returned by the second party, a process which may take up to several days. In other cases, documents may take days, weeks or even months to negotiate and conclude. This is especially true for guarantees, ISDA agreements and collateral/margining agreements in support of derivatives activity, or credit agreements supporting loans or other credit facilities. In such cases legal risk exposure may last considerably longer, but must be resolved as soon as practicable; only then can operational and legal risks be reduced or eliminated.

7.33 ESTABLISHING DOCUMENTARY TARGETS AND THRESHOLDS CAN HELP LIMIT OPERATIONAL AND LEGAL RISKS; INCOMPLETE DOCUMENTATION SHOULD BE PRIORITIZED BY CREDITWORTHINESS AND RISK EXPOSURE

In order to help minimize the operational and legal risks arising from delayed execution of relevant documents, a firm can consider establishing business-specific documentation targets; this can help contain the maximum risk exposure arising from lack of documentation. For instance, if a fixed income desk engaged in repurchase agreements has 100 documented clients and 25 undocumented clients, the legal and risk functions may decide that a minimum of 10 signed agreements must be delivered each month. Failure to meet the targets may result in curtailment of credit-sensitive trading with those that remain undocumented, or the levy of a financial penalty on sales/trading desks for each day or week the documents remain past due. Alternatively, in order to limit the risk exposure generated by incomplete legal documentation, the governance bodies may wish to place dollar exposure caps on the amount of business that can be transacted while documentation is still "in progress." Once that cap is reached, no further business can be conducted until more of the backlog is eliminated. In cases where a great deal of documentation is chronically overdue, credit and market risk officers should help the legal and operational departments prioritize the task by creditworthiness and risk exposure. Thus, weaker credits should become priorities, since they have a greater probability of defaulting over the near-term (precisely when legal documentation is most necessary). Equally, credits with a great deal of exposure should become priorities; though they are less likely to default, the sheer magnitude of exposure may cause significant financial problems for the firm should the "unthinkable" actually occur. Regardless of the specific approach followed, the risk committee and board should be apprised of risks posed by unexecuted documents.

Summarizing the simple rules associated with the ongoing management of risks, we note the following:

- Many of the qualitative aspects of the discipline come into play when trying to create a strong management framework; indeed, effective management relates to common sense, communication, visibility and discipline.
- Prudent management of risk means focusing intently on liquidity issues — being conservative when evaluating and managing the risk parameters of any risk that can impact on- and off-balance sheet operations.
- Since liquidity is the essence of financial management, care must be taken to ensure assets and liabilities are protected against illiquidity; this means implementing objective reserve mechanisms, using conservative assumptions when applying liquidation horizons, developing diversified funding sources, establishing financial incentives and penalties to reduce illiquid assets, and so on.
- Effective management also centers on disciplined, well-organized risk-taking — within risk classes and specialties rather than across them — and strong, client-focused sales practices that treat end-users with respect and care.

- All risks must be included in official trading systems, without exception; failure to do so leaves a firm subject to operational risks and possible fraud.
- Risk mitigation/migration devices form part of the management process, and should be used whenever it makes sense to do so.
- Legal processes, based on appropriate documentation, should exist as a key element of the management discipline in order to reduce, or eliminate, legal/operational risk losses.

8

Risk Infrastructure

Risk infrastructure makes possible the identification, quantification, reporting and management of risks. Though infrastructure is often "invisible" to those outside of the risk function — encompassing "behind the scenes" data, technology and internal analytics — it is a vital element of the risk process. Indeed, in the absence of solid infrastructure a firm is unlikely to be able to satisfy its internal/external obligations and fiduciary requirements, or convince shareholders, creditors and regulators that it is operating in a controlled manner. Though the development of an appropriate layer of infrastructure can be complex, time-consuming and expensive, there is often no substitute or alternative. Financial business is so complicated that it is no longer practical to manage risks without proper infrastructure; a solid, committed and well-planned infrastructure investment is therefore a requirement. Reliance on an outdated, manual or inflexible platform may ultimately lead to a greater amount of operating risks and financial losses.

8.1 DATA IS THE FUNDAMENTAL COMPONENT OF ANY RISK PROCESS — BAD DATA LEADS TO BAD INFORMATION AND BAD RISK DECISIONS

Information makes the management of risk possible. Data, the basic component of any information process, is the fundamental mechanism used to convey details about the nature, size, location and maturity of a firm's risks. Large firms that operate many lines of business, with multiple counterparties in various global locations, face a considerable challenge in ensuring that risk data is of the highest possible quality; however, even small firms need to implement processes that ensure data integrity. Bad data will, in many cases, lead to bad (or misinformed) risk decisions. If a firm's data processes cannot reflect basic information — such as whether a business is long or short, owns \$1MM or \$10MM of risk, or faces Bank XYZ or Bank ABC as counterparty — then risk decisions cannot be made with confidence. Data must be correct at the position, or trade, level. Since risks are often aggregated into broader portfolios — whether by counterparty, region, entity or risk class — a data error at the position level can have significant consequences; not only will portfolio information be incorrect, but error identification is likely to be time-consuming. A robust data process therefore relies heavily on integrity at the position level. Time and effort must be spent converting trade data into clean and robust form, and processes must exist to maintain the quality of the process.

Though every firm has unique data needs, most share certain common requirements; these may include business unit, desk, trade size, trade type (e.g. swap, put, call, bond, equity, and so forth), security identifier (e.g. a unique tag in order to avoid duplication or mismatch errors), maturity, counterparty currency, country, industry, settlement time, documentation flags (e.g. for confirmations, ISDAs, guarantees, and so on), and so forth. Such data permits the computation of core credit, market and liquidity exposures. In some cases trading systems apply risk analytics to each position to derive actual exposures; in other cases "raw" data is ported to the independent risk function, where internal risk analytics compute relevant risks. Regardless of where the risk calculations are performed, aggregation and netting rules must then be applied in order to construct actual portfolios of risks.

The data process developed must be flexible enough to accommodate new products, counterparties, markets and analytics, and an audit cycle should exist to ensure integrity. These are obvious, if sometimes overlooked, elements of the process. Since the pace of change in the financial markets is so rapid, any "data capture" mechanism that is not sufficiently flexible will soon become obsolete — putting a firm back where it started. Likewise, failure to audit the process on an ongoing basis could mean that new products are not captured appropriately, spurious information is produced and left unchecked, and so forth. Earlier in the book we noted that hiring the best, most experienced and qualified risk personnel is a worthwhile investment in a firm's risk process and overall financial future. Investing in data processes must rank as a close second; spending the time and resources to develop a robust data process leads ultimately to more informed decision-making and safer risk-taking.

The availability of high quality information — built on robust data processes — is of such importance that it becomes one of the "cardinal rules."

8.2 A SINGLE SOURCE OF TRADE DATA SHOULD BE USED WHENEVER POSSIBLE TO ENSURE CONSISTENCY; WHEN THIS IS NOT POSSIBLE, DATA PROCESSES MUST BE PROPERLY RECONCILED AND AUDITED

One of the most common "information problems" comes from the use of multiple sources of data to produce similar, or identical, management and risk reports. When multiple sources are employed for reporting purposes, it is often impossible to create the same end-use information; this is especially true when complex businesses are involved. For reasons of corporate history, a firm may use multiple trade repositories for different aspects of financial processing. Thus, one database might contain a trade population used to produce risk information, a second for P&L generation, a third for settlements, a fourth for collateral valuation, and so on. In addition, for complicated businesses where the standard trade platform cannot handle difficult structures, spreadsheets might be used to manage a portion of the management/reporting task. Under this type of structure, it becomes necessary to reconcile multiple sources of information; since it is of little use to compute P&L explain from the finance database if the risk database does not feature the same trade population, reconciliation is a necessary procedure. The best way of gaining confidence in the quality of information is to obtain all data from the same source. However, many institutions are burdened with legacy systems and cannot realistically obtain their risk information from a single data source. In the short-term the only practical solution is to institute as many audit checks as possible; this, however, must only be regarded as a "stop-gap" measure. With the advent of new technologies it has become more realistic to consider and implement a cohesive data platform that contains all business data (risk, finance, operations, settlement, legal, counterparty, management, and so on) and becomes the sole source of information for any control or business function. Firms that have not yet considered such architecture may be delaying the inevitable and should prioritize their efforts — particularly since information demands are likely to increase in the future.

8.3 TECHNOLOGY SHOULD BE MADE AS FLEXIBLE AS POSSIBLE IN ORDER TO ACCOMMODATE THE CHANGING BUSINESS ENVIRONMENT

The financial markets are extremely dynamic — new markets open, new products are created and new clients begin dealing, trading or borrowing; with deregulation and globalization, this dynamism will continue to accelerate. Since firms creating or using new instruments or employing new risk and financing techniques are likely to remain active in new structures, the underlying technology they use to deal, process, settle, clear and report business must be extremely flexible. The inflexibility of legacy systems introduced in the 1980s and 1990s is an issue that continues to burden many institutions. Technology processes implemented before the mid-1990s were often rigid and focused only on what needed to be done at the time — often with little allowance for future product changes. Firms that continue to operate on such platforms encounter these limitations and must deal with the business risks they generate. With the advent of flexible programming languages and technology interfaces, business, trading and risk platforms have become far more accommodating; firms that embrace such technology are able to reduce their operational risks.

Given the dynamic nature of the financial markets, it is virtually impossible for a particular element of a firm's risk infrastructure — analytics, data, technology, policy, and so forth — to remain completely up to date without flexible architecture. Firms must therefore plan for, and implement, such flexible infrastructure; for most firms this is likely to be a multi-year task that should be approached in discrete steps. Since infrastructure solutions are often expensive and consume valuable corporate resources, there is little sense in planning a multi-year infrastructure project without interim deliverables and check-points. Project managers need to ensure that solutions are delivered according to a pre-agreed schedule, and that performance penalties accrue to those failing to deliver required functionality. Thus, if a firm is developing a new risk exposure analytics suite designed to accommodate any instrument with a cash flow (making it enormously flexible and capable of handling "next generation" products that have not yet been created) it should approach the project in measurable stages. For instance, it may decide that its first six-month phase will center on the creation of a new risk data template; 12 months after that it will introduce new potential credit exposure methodologies; after that, a new market risk module, with alternate VAR methodologies, will go into production; and so forth. It is vital for any plan to include measurable goals and deadlines that create accountability and momentum.

8.4 RISK REQUIREMENTS SHOULD BE A CENTRAL PART OF ANY BUSINESS TECHNOLOGY BLUEPRINT

It is essential that risk requirements be included in the design or upgrade of any technology platform. Since risk takers and risk officers have very specific requirements related to the information and functionality required to monitor and manage risks (including items that impact those in the internal governance structure, as well as regulators and external auditors), their input is essential. Other control functions, such as audit, legal, treasury and finance, must incorporate their own requirements in any platform change as well; where requirements overlap, such as in P&L explain or collateral valuation functionality, they should be aligned and agreed in advance. Formal approval by a member of the governance structure (e.g. the risk committee) is also advisable; indeed, given the considerable amount of resources devoted to technology issues the creation of a technology sub-committee, that operates under the jurisdiction of the risk committee, may be warranted. Such a sub-committee can review and critique risk technology proposals and ensure consistency in strategic direction.

8.5 TECHNOLOGY CHANGES THAT IMPACT RISK MANAGEMENT, FINANCE, LEGAL, REGULATORY REPORTING AND OPERATIONS SHOULD ALWAYS BE CONSIDERED JOINTLY

An extension of the rule above relates to coordination across control functions whenever joint technology changes are involved. Control functions typically seek to quantify, measure and track information pertinent to their specific disciplines. While most functionality (i.e. perhaps 75% or more) can be considered independently — that is, independent of any other control unit — certain core functionality can directly impact other units; in such cases, proper coordination is essential. For instance, if the finance department is contemplating a change in its P&L reporting process (perhaps it is reclassifying accounts or changing the structural hierarchy of business units/departments) it must remember that any change in P&L reporting will affect the market risk management function. Market risk officers, implementing the firm's VAR process and needing to perform historic backtesting of P&L against VAR, need to be consulted in advance of such changes — if the VAR measure is not synchronized with the P&L function, backtesting of results will fail. Likewise, if the legal department wants to change how it implements and views netting agreements, it should do so in consultation with credit officers, who will also be affected by the change. One area likely to be impacted by virtually any change is the official regulatory reporting function; since much of what a regulatory reporting function produces for regulators has to conform to specific regulatory standards, reporting changes requested by risk officers, controllers, auditors or business managers should not be implemented unilaterally — prior consultation with regulatory reporting experts is essential.

8.6 MINIMUM STANDARDS RELATED TO RISK TECHNOLOGY, ANALYTICS AND REPORTING SHOULD BE APPLIED TO ALL RISK-TAKING BUSINESS

Firms often give individual trading desks and business units a reasonable amount of freedom in designing technology, analytics and reporting modules in support of their business. This is logical, as each business has idiosyncratic requirements and must be able to control and manage exposures in the most effective manner possible. A technology, analytics and reporting platform that is appropriate for an internal corporate treasury function managing the firm's interest rate and currency exposure may be inappropriate for an equity derivative desk structuring complex deals for sophisticated end-users; each needs unique functionality. Preserving the individual character and requirements of each unit is thus an important component of effective business and risk management. That said, certain minimum standards must be applied throughout a firm in order to avoid communication and management problems. These standards help ensure that when a central process or policy needs to be applied, individual units can immediately conform. It also helps eliminate "cross-system" communication problems that often plague legacy architecture. For example, if every business unit is required to submit a particular set of daily risk information in a prespecified format, the individual technology and analytic platforms must be capable of presenting information as required. If certain standard regulatory reports are required (e.g. large counterparty credit exposures which detail future exposure, net mark-to-market and collateral value), then each unit should be capable of submitting the information requested. By adhering to common standards a firm is positioned to compute and convey its risk profile quickly and efficiently; as business complexity increases, application of standards becomes even more important. Over the medium-term, a plan for unified, scalable and flexible technology (with relevant analytic and reporting features) remains the single best way of ensuring firm-wide standards are met.

8.7 A RISK CONTROL SYSTEM IS NOT A RISK MANAGEMENT SYSTEM; THE TWO ARE DIFFERENT AND BOTH ARE NECESSARY

Although independent risk officers and business managers (whether traders, bankers or salespeople) often have similar aims when it comes to viewing and managing risk, they often have unique technology requirements. Risk officers typically require functionality that is characteristic of what might be termed a "risk control system." That is, they need a platform that delivers, at the end of each business day, predefined risk information in sufficient detail to provide a relevant picture of the firm's credit, market and liquidity risks. The system does not necessarily have to be real-time, or provide the same amount of trade-level detail characteristic of a risk management system. In general, risk control systems do not feature risk analytics to compute risk sensitivities, stress scenarios, future credit exposure, or other risk measures; rather, they tend to receive information from underlying risk management platforms, and aggregate trades or portfolios by counterparty, market, risk class, region, legal entity, and so on. The aggregation feature is vital as it helps identify firm-wide exposures, including concentrations. A risk control system generally features limit monitoring capabilities in order to automate aspects of the monitoring, reporting and violation process.

A risk management system, in contrast, is effectively a trading platform with a considerable amount of risk functionality. In many cases the platform is business- or product-specific (though new technologies now allow greater flexibility, interaction and scalability, meaning many lines of business can be accommodated). Risk management systems must generally capture the effects of changing markets and trading positions on a real-time basis, and are often equipped with specific pricing and analytic tools required to produce risk sensitivities, stress scenarios, credit exposures, and so on; such functionality allows for dynamic pricing and risk management. Since the platforms are effectively trade-entry mechanisms, they contain very detailed trade information — far more detailed than might be encountered in a typical risk control platform. Indeed, risk management systems are generally the source of trade data for a firm's official books and records and, per the rule above, are central to the data integrity process. Risk management systems often have middle and back-office functionality (or links to such modules), allowing for straight-through processing of trades with minimal human intervention. Importantly, risk management systems must have the capability of communicating with risk control systems; this permits information to be transmitted and allows the risk control system to act as a firm's total risk aggregator. Thus, while risk control systems and risk management systems share certain common features, they are fundamentally different platforms — one should not be expected to do the work of the other, but both are required in order to ensure a solid risk infrastructure. A risk control system tends to be a static, non-real-time risk aggregator/monitor that acts as a recipient of risk data — a firm should not, therefore, expect it to act as a real-time platform with extensive computational capabilities. A risk management system tends to be a dynamic, real-time, trade-entry platform and feeder; it may be business-specific (or used for several businesses) and is unlikely, in most cases, to be capable of aggregating all of a firm's risk.

8.8 THE TECHNOLOGY PLATFORM THAT GENERATES VALUATIONS AND RISK INFORMATION MUST BE UNDER THE SCRUTINY/CONTROL OF TECHNOLOGICAL AUDITORS/RISK MANAGERS

As indicated earlier, a true risk management system may be used for multiple purposes, including trade-entry, pricing, risk analytics, mid-office valuation and back-end settlement and reporting. In cases where the platform is integrated and used for both trade-entry and risk management, it is important that the underlying code, and processes generated by the code, be under the supervision and control of an independent function. This approach — which is designed to prevent traders or business managers from accessing and manipulating any code that might impact valuations and risk parameters — helps ensure integrity of the process. The most obvious "guardians" of the technology platform are likely to come from an independent information technology group, a technology audit organization, or a technology arm of the independent risk management function. In addition to remaining under the control of an independent party, code changes should be well documented, and separate version control that automatically logs code changes should be made available to relevant control and business units. Under no circumstances should the front-office have the ability to change code; this represents a breach of the independence rule and creates a flaw in the control structure. When code is not independently maintained the effects can be damaging. For instance, in the Barings case, Leeson was able to instruct outside technologists to change the programming code related to risk reporting so that key management risk reports generated by the system were suppressed.

8.9 CHANGES IN RISK MEASURES, PROCESSES OR TECHNOLOGY BY THE TRADING OR RISK MANAGEMENT FUNCTIONS MUST BE THOROUGHLY DEVELOPED, TESTED, REVIEWED AND DOCUMENTED BEFORE BEING IMPLEMENTED

Given the dynamism of the financial business it comes as no surprise that risk measures, analytics and processes must occasionally be enhanced or modified. Changes might be required as a result of the introduction of new products or business lines, the creation of more efficient risk management and pricing models, the development of new hedging/risk management techniques, the arrival of new competitors, the implementation of new technology modules, and so on. While enhancements are a natural sign of progress, care must be taken to ensure they occur in a controlled environment. Altering any measurement or pricing algorithm, for instance, should be done in a rigorous fashion; this might include documenting the new approach, testing it under multiple scenarios through the technology platform, commissioning internal/external peer reviews and preparing detailed technical specifications. Thus, if a trading desk is altering the way it prices long-dated currency options, or if the market risk unit is changing its implementation of VAR, the new techniques should be subjected to the very highest standards of testing, peer review and documentation. In order to ensure proper governance, the risk committee should formally review and approve any substantive changes; this is especially critical when it involves information that might be communicated to shareholders, rating agencies or regulators (such as a change in methodology or policy).

8.10 USE OF SHORT-TERM, TEMPORARY INFRASTRUCTURE SOLUTIONS IS ACCEPTABLE, BUT THESE SHOULD BE REPLACED BY ROBUST SOLUTIONS AS SOON AS POSSIBLE

In practice, firms operating in the financial markets are likely to feature some form of data, analytics, policy, reporting and technology infrastructure. This infrastructure may be automated or manual, sophisticated or crude, trade- or portfolio-centric, and product- or market-based. In reality, few large firms possess "ideal" infrastructure (e.g. a platform that handles all dimensions of current and expected business, with proper control and automation); this does not mean that a firm should not strive to implement such infrastructure. However, since a firm must still operate a business while it implements infrastructure improvement plans, it may have to make do with temporary infrastructure solutions for some of its business lines. Such solutions may not be as efficient or automated as desired, and they may be prone to error. In the absence of the "ideal" infrastructure solution, however, temporary measures are better than none at all — they do, after all, provide a modicum of control. When infrastructure solutions are known to have weaknesses, audit procedures should be instituted to monitor errors or problems. This emerges as a practical solution to the daunting challenge of having to overhaul, enhance, build or replace all aspects of risk infrastructure. That said, it is very important that temporary infrastructure solutions do not become "permanent," particularly when they are not robust and efficient. Settling for the "status quo" breeds complacency and exposes the firm to new, or incremental, operating risks as business grows or changes. For instance, if a firm needs to make use of spreadsheet-based technology solutions to track the valuation and risk of a small, complex derivative book (that is simply too intricate to be accommodated by the firm's standard derivative system) it may be acceptable as a short-term measure, particularly if the number of transactions is small and auditors and controllers can police the process. It becomes unacceptable, however, if that temporary spreadsheet solution remains in place for months or years as the de-facto "permanent" mechanism for booking and tracking complex derivative exposures. In this case the firm is likely to encounter various infrastructure control issues related to the integrity of data, accuracy of analytics and soundness of valuation. At a minimum, a firm that employs temporary infrastructure solutions should require business and control officers to submit a plan for moving to a more robust environment — and hold them accountable for achieving the goal.

8.11 WHEN AUTOMATED INFRASTRUCTURE SOLUTIONS ARE NOT AVAILABLE, THE BEST MANUAL SOLUTIONS, WITH CHECKS AND BALANCES, SHOULD BE IMPLEMENTED

Continuing with the theme above, it is not always possible for a firm to immediately implement automated technology solutions. Such an "ideal world" is not a practical reality for all organizations, as the time, resources and financial constraints can be too large to justify the benefits — at least in the short-term. When ideal solutions are not available, a firm may wish to pursue two parallel courses: implementing the best "manual" solutions and developing a short to medium-term plan that allows it to gradually migrate to more automated processes. Implementing the best possible manual solutions requires two additional steps: advising those in the governance structure that certain aspects of the firm's infrastructure are manual and unlikely to be as robust and efficient as desired — this provides them with due notice that operational risk problems could arise; and requiring that manual processes be reviewed by controllers and auditors on a regular basis to help capture any potential weaknesses. An over-reliance on manual processes leads to increased probability of human error and a corresponding increase in operational risk losses; protecting against this through checks and balances is a necessary requirement while automated processes are being developed. For instance, if a firm wishes to execute several manually intensive loan transactions and lacks the technology to do so, it may seek approval to conduct its business on a manual basis. This may involve manual preparation and processing of loan documents, manual preparation of payment instructions for periodic coupons, and so forth. If the risk committee is aware of this manual "workaround" it may sanction the execution of several loan trades while an automated solution is being developed; the financial controller responsible for the business may perform additional checks and reviews to ensure ongoing data integrity. In order to remain disciplined, however, a firm should not permit temporary manually intensive business to continue without a permanent automation solution.

8.12 "OFF-THE-SHELF" TECHNOLOGY SOLUTIONS THAT PROVIDE 80% OR 90% OF THE CAPABILITY A FIRM IS SEEKING CAN BE AN IDEAL SOLUTION

Over the past few decades it has not been unusual for large financial and corporate firms, with a broad range of business lines spanning the globe, to feature very large, and dedicated, information technology (IT) departments responsible for creating the infrastructure to conduct business. Many departments have elected to "build" rather than "buy" the necessary data, analytics and technology required to support businesses, under the assumption that they can more readily address the unique needs of their business and control users. While this may be an effective approach for certain companies, it has not proven beneficial for all; some firms have been unable to manage their IT resources efficiently and have spent considerable amounts of money on projects that have not worked out as planned. With the arrival of flexible technologies, many outside vendors have done a good job of creating "off-the-shelf" solutions that meet the broad requirements of many firms. Indeed, certain products and services offered by leading vendors have enough capability and flexibility to give interested firms coverage of the majority of their requirements. When a firm is able to identify an "off-the-shelf" infrastructure solution — covering data templates, analytics and technology processing (trade-entry, mid-office valuation/risk reporting and back-office settlement and clearing) — that is customizable, flexible and scalable, it must consider the time and effort that can be saved over the "internal build" route. While very few standard packages/solutions can offer 100% of a firm's desired functionality, those that can provide a large majority — say, 80% or more — can be extremely attractive. What a firm gives up in total coverage of requirements, it can save in time and money; in addition, it implements a more secure control environment much more rapidly, a feature that could allow it to prevent losses.

8.13 INFRASTRUCTURE CONTINGENCY PLANS SHOULD TAKE ACCOUNT OF ALL RISK REQUIREMENTS

As noted in Chapter 3, when disaster strikes a business site, pre-planned contingency response must move into effect immediately. This means that any technological infrastructure needed to support the daily processing of business flows, including front-end trade entry, middle and back-office functionality, basic control reporting and data back-up, must be ready to take over for downed systems. A central core of this infrastructure plan should include risk-related analytics and reporting that allow a firm to know its risks at the time of the crisis, and to engage in basic business (or at least risk mitigation) for the duration of the crisis. Since business and control managers cannot know when disaster will strike, they need to be able to reconstruct their risk positions before the start of the next day's market opening. This means that all risk and financial information must be stored in duplicate in an offsite location at the end of each business day. As part of the contingency planning process, it is also critical for alternate trading, middle and back-office, and risk control systems to be regularly tested for access and functionality. Indeed, a firm's entire contingency planning process should be tested regularly, to ensure that it operates as intended precisely when needed. Solid crisis management on the technology front must, of course, be accompanied by planning related to key personnel. All "front line" critical personnel involved with business generation, risk management, control and settlements must be familiar with the contingency plan, how to access remote business locations and how to make use of back-up technology platforms. They should also be familiar with the suite of reports and information that will be available — this is particularly critical if the offsite location is not a precise "mirror image" of the normal business technology platform, but a scaled-down version with more limited functionality.

Summarizing the simple rules of infrastructure, we note the following:

- A risk process will often succeed, or fail, based on the quality of the underlying technological infrastructure and, more specifically, the quality of the data.
- Data, which provides the risk and business functions with information needed to conduct business and manage risk, must be well-defined, clean and robust, and flow from a single source; appropriate audit checks should surround the data process to ensure ongoing integrity.
- Minimum risk technology and data standards must be applied throughout the firm to ensure consistency.
- Technology platforms (including underlying code governing analytics) must be under the control of independent parties.
- Risk platforms must always be as flexible as possible — since the financial markets change, the technology supporting activities must be able to change in tandem.
- While robust technology solutions are a necessary goal, business realities mean that temporary solutions must be accommodated — under strict controls, and with a view towards developing more durable solutions.
- Any changes in risk infrastructure, including technologies, methodologies, and so on, must be thoroughly tested and documented in a proper test environment before being implemented.
- Infrastructure contingency plans are an essential component of risk management — a firm must be able to continue its risk-taking and risk management activities without pause in the event of a disruption.

9 Summary

Throughout this text we have endeavored to present simple rules that we believe are crucial to the creation of an effective risk management process. As noted, many of the rules are based on collective risk management experience drawn from the marketplace. Crises, dislocations and process failures that have occurred over the past few decades (and over the past few years, in particular) provide valuable lessons for all institutions. Those who follow the lessons can improve their control processes — there are certainly enough "real life" examples to demonstrate how processes can be strengthened in order to avoid, or minimize, risk-related problems. Those who choose to ignore them do so at their own peril: for example, if a firm chooses not to create an independent risk function or separate front and back-office duties, it is ignoring the lessons of LTCM, Barings, Sumitomo Corporation and Daiwa Bank; if a bank chooses not to apply prudent credit lending and collateral standards when financing speculative projects, it is ignoring the lessons of the Japanese banking sector during the speculative bubble of the 1990s; if a firm does not properly account for the shortcomings of models, it is ignoring the lessons of National Westminster Bank and Bank of Tokyo Mitsubishi; if a firm opts not to take account of liquidity risk and collateral liquidation during stressed market conditions, it is ignoring the experience of hedge funds and large international investment banks during the 1998 Russian crisis.

Many of the rules that we have presented emphasize logical and prudent approaches to considering and managing risks; while the quantitative dimension of risk is of vital importance (and must never be ignored) it has been our aim to stress the importance of the "common sense" considerations that are occasionally forgotten or de-emphasized. We believe that firms actively taking risk should be extremely careful not to overlook this qualitative dimension. Some of the risk rules we have discussed are simple in concept and easy to implement; they require very little incremental effort and virtually no resources, but can add considerable control value. For instance, requiring managers to know the skills and behaviors of their risk takers, recognizing that large positions can create liquidity-induced losses, ensuring risk officers are always available for consultation, or requiring new products to be considered and approved by an independent new product committee are all examples of simple, but effective, steps that can be taken without burdening a firm's resources. Others may be simple to understand but more complicated to put in place, and may require considerable human, financial or technology resource commitments. Since they add value they are likely to be worth the incremental effort and resources, though each firm must engage in its own cost/benefit analysis and make that determination. For instance, creating proper risk data templates, building flexible trading and risk technology, or staffing a risk function with experienced professionals are all examples of rules that are simple in concept and valuable from a control perspective, but which are likely to require additional financial and human resources. Regardless of the complexity of implementation, the risk management process should incorporate as many of these rules as possible. At a minimum, adherence to what we have termed the "cardinal rules" is advisable. By implementing the cardinal rules, a firm can strengthen key elements of the process and so gain greater confidence in continuing, or expanding, risk-taking activities. Implementation of the cardinal rules, or any of the broader rules we have presented, requires management support; without a "top down" management push to create a strong risk culture based on fundamental risk rules, a firm's control process will never be as strong as it can, or should, be. Management must be completely committed to creating a strong risk process.

As we have discussed, a risk process must be driven by a clear and concise philosophy that delineates and defines all risk-taking activities. For some firms risk-bearing is a minor component of overall business, with risks that should be minimized or eliminated whenever possible. For others it forms the bulk of activities and revenues; in such cases a robust and dynamic risk process is essential. Once a philosophy exists, a risk governance structure can be created; this empowers groups and individuals within an organization to develop, implement and maintain the risk process. Effective risk governance creates authority, responsibility and accountability, and helps ensure that risk-taking does not occur in a vacuum. Once a governance framework has been created, a risk control process can be built, or expanded, around the core disciplines of identification, quantification, monitoring and management. While each of these sectors requires attention and resources, the basic rules applicable to each are straightforward, and based heavily on common sense, prudence, judgment and experience. The entire risk process must be flexible and dynamic; as financial markets and associated risks change, a control process must be able to change in tandem.

- The identification phase focuses on understanding, in detail, the specific risk exposures being contemplated. Risks must be understood and identified before they can be managed.
- The quantification phase — where quantitative and qualitative approaches to risk management intersect — assigns a financial value to exposures that have been identified; without assigning such a value, it is impossible to determine how much might be gained or lost through risk activities. Quantification also permits allocation of capital and establishment of risk limits to control exposures.
- The monitoring phase permits risk exposures to be tracked and reported; this allows internal and external parties to understand the scope and magnitude of risk activities. Monitoring also ensures compliance with limits and policies enacted by governance bodies.
- The management phase allows for ongoing risk decisions and exposure adjustments; this ensures all available tools, techniques, skills and experience are used to actively manage the risks of the business.
- Risk infrastructure surrounds the entire process. Such infrastructure permits the practical measurement, monitoring and management of risk; the more advanced and flexible the infrastructure, the simpler the task of gathering, analyzing and transmitting risk information. This does not mean the management of risk is any easier, it simply means that gaining access to the information required to manage risk is easier — saving time and resources, and allowing decisions to be made with greater confidence.

It is important to re-emphasize that a risk process must draw in quantitative processes whenever necessary; quantitative tools are an important dimension of risk management — forming an essential element of the qualitative/quantitative risk partnership — and should be actively used. Though certain mathematical tools have limitations and can expose a firm to specific risks, they provide information that makes possible the practical management of risk.

Ultimately, the key to the "simple rules of risk" is remembering the lessons of history. The financial markets contain many examples of institutions that failed to implement, or follow, relatively basic rules of risk process and management. By remaining disciplined in creating, and adhering to, a comprehensive risk process, a firm that actively assumes risk can prosper.

Selected References

Association of Finance Professionals, "Principles and Practices for the Oversight and Management of Financial Risk," AFP: New York (1998).

Bank for International Settlements, "Operational Risk Management," Basel Committee Publications No. 42: Basel (1998).

Bank for International Settlements, "Report on OTC Derivatives: Settlement Procedures and Counterparty Risk Management," CPSS Publications No. 27: Basel (1998).

Bank for International Settlements, "Recommendations for Public Disclosure of Trading and Derivatives Activities of Banks and Securities Firms," Basel Committee Publications No. 48: Basel (1999).

Bank for International Settlements, "Credit Risk Modeling," Basel Committee Publications No. 49: Basel (1999).

Bank for International Settlements, "A Survey of Stress Tests and Current Practice at Financial Institutions," Basel Committee Publications, April 2001.

Banks, E., *The Credit Risk of Complex Derivatives*, 2nd Ed., Macmillan: London (1996).

Basel Committee on Banking Supervision, "Sound Practices of Managing Liquidity in Banking Organizations," Basel Committee Publications: Basel (2000).

Beder, T.S., "VAR: Seductive but Dangerous," Financial Analysts Journal, September–October 1995.

Cagan, P., "The First Gentle Steps," Futures and Options World, February 2002, pp. 48–51.

Caouette, J., E. Altman and P. Narayanan, *Managing Credit Risk*, John Wiley: New York (1998).

Carey, M., "Dimensions of Credit Risk and their Relationship to Economic Capital Requirements," Federal Reserve Board, March 15, 2000.

Celarier, M., "How the Banks Caught Hedge Fund Fever," Global Finance, March 1994, pp. 48–53.

Chew, L., *Managing Derivative Risks*, John Wiley: New York (1996).

Counterparty Risk Management Policy Group, "Improving Counterparty Risk Management Practices," June 1999, New York.

Crouhy, M., R. Mark and D. Galai, *Managing Risk*, McGraw-Hill: New York (2000).

Das, S., "Liquidity Risk," Futures and Options World, February 2002, pp. 55–62.

Decker, P., "The Changing Character of Liquidity and Liquidity Risk Management: A Regulator's Perspective," Federal Reserve Bank of Chicago, April 2000.

Derivatives Policy Group, " Framework for Voluntary Oversight," DPG: New York (1995).

Diamond, D. and R. Rajan, "Liquidity Risk, Liquidity Creation and Financial Fragility: A Theory of Banking," University of Chicago Working Paper No. 476, July 1998.

Dowd, K., J. Aragones and C. Blanco, "Incorporating Stress Tests into Market Risk Modeling," Derivatives Quarterly, Spring 2001, Vol. 7, No. 3.

Duffie, D. and A. Ziegler, "Liquidity Risk," Stanford University Working Paper, August 2001.

Garman, M., "Taking VAR to Pieces," Risk Magazine, October 1997, pp. 70–71.

Giegerich, U., "How Companies can Use VAR Models," The Treasurer, January 1997, pp. 29–32.

Group of 30, Global Derivatives Study Group, *Derivatives: Practices and Principles*, G30: Washington, D.C. (1993).

Hoppe, R., "VAR and the Unreal World," Risk Magazine, July 1998, pp. 45–50.

International Organization of Securities Commissions, "Risk Management and Control Guidance for Securities Firms and their Supervisors," IOSCO: Basel (1998).

Jorion, P., "How Long Term Lost its Capital," Risk, September 1999, pp. 31–36.

Jorion, P., *Value-at-Risk*, 2nd Ed., McGraw-Hill: New York (2000).

Kimball, R., "Failures in Risk Management," New England Economic Review, January–February 2000.

King, J., *Operational Risk: Measurement and Modeling*, John Wiley: New York (2001).

Office of the Comptroller of the Currency, "OCC Bulletin 2000-16, Risk Modeling," OCC: Washington, D.C. (May 2000).

Scholes, M., "Crisis and Risk Management," Risk, May 2000, pp. 50–53.

Schwartz, R. and C. Smith, *Derivatives Handbook: Risk Management and Control*, John Wiley: New York (1997).

Shepheard-Walwyn, T. and R. Litterman, "Building a Coherent Risk Measurement and Capital Optimization Model for Financial Firms," Federal Reserve Bank of New York Economic Policy Review, October 1998, pp. 171–182.

Shireff, D., "The Eve of Destruction," Euromoney, November 1998, pp. 34–36.

Smith, C., "Is Disclosure in the Balance?" Futures and Options World, May 2001, pp. 45–48.

Smithson, C., "Firmwide Risk: How Firms are Integrating Risk Management," Risk, March 1997, p. 10.

Smithson, C., *Managing Financial Risk*, 3rd Ed., McGraw-Hill: New York (1998).

Stein, J., "The Integration of Market and Credit Risk Measurement," Financial Engineering News, November 1998.

Taleb, N., *Dynamic Hedging*, John Wiley: New York (1996).

Tomasula, D., "Plugging the Holes in Risk Systems," Wall Street and Technology, 1996, Vol. 14, pp. 45–47.

Wendel, C., "The New Face of Credit Risk Management," RMA Publications: New York (1999).

Index